Brighid's Healing

Gina McGarry

Green Magic

This edition is published by

Green Magic
Long Barn
Sutton Mallet
TA7 9AR
England
www.greenmagicpublishing.com

Typeset by Academic + Technical, Bristol

Cover design: Chris Render
Cover illustration: Jane Brideson
Technical assistance: Guy Gotto
Cover production: Kay Hayden
k.design@virgin.net

ISBN 0 9547 2302 3

Reprinted 2007

GREEN MAGIC

CONTENTS

DEDICATION

A good laugh and a long sleep are the
best cures in the doctor's book.

Irish proverb

Three medicines – Water, honey, labour

Druidical Triad

Ta luibh ar gach leighas
There is a herb for every ailment

Nil luibh gan leighas
There is not a herb without a cure

From a manuscript written in 1352:

'May the merciful God have mercy on us all. I have here collected practical rules from several works for the honour of God, for the benefit of the
Irish people, and for the love of my friends and kindred... These are
things gentle, sweet, profitable and of little evil, things which have
often been tested by us and our instructors. I pray God to bless those
(doctors) who will use this book and I lay it on their souls as a conjuration,
that they extract not sparingly from it; that they fail not on account of
neglecting the practical rules herein contained, and more especially that
they do their duty in cases where they receive no pay on account of
the poverty of the patients...'

INTRODUCTION

Brighid's blessings upon you! It will be a joy to travel along the path of the Celtic healer with you! It is always such a wondrous privilege to pass on the collected wisdom of our ancestors and it is my prayer that this book inspires and empowers you to deepen your own relationship with nature and the healing traditions of our Ancient Ones.

I'm a big believer in making things as simple as possible and I also believe that it is more empowering to teach people how to ask the right questions, rather than just giving them a bunch of answers (there are all kinds of people who will give you answers, whether they're right for you or not!), so my writing style tends to be more 'streamlined' than some of the wordier tomes out there. There is a great power in words. They can be keys that open doorways to whole worlds of wisdom. Therefore, much of your work will entail the contemplation of key words and concepts – what do they mean to *you*? What do they conjure, what do they connect *you* to? There will be facts to memorise, of course, based on science and historical experience, particularly in the subjects of Anatomy, Physiology and *Materia Medica*, but I never want to get bogged down in facts so much that we lose sense or Spirit and the Individual.

This book contains words of power for you to contemplate your relationship to and awareness of. A journal would be a good way to record your revelations. Endeavour to stay flexible, there are many truths and hardly anything is written in stone! We want to avoid going fanatical about anything!

The following is an example of what I mean – the herbs, attitudes and archetypes listed below are each a healing modality in and of itself, each working in its own way as a 'simple' *and* they can be woven together into holistic formulas to suit individual needs. Just as there are many herbs for any one condition, so are there many aspects of Spirit that would aid in the healing process, depending on the individual. It is important to stay open to all kinds or miraculous possibilities.

So, begin by contemplating your relationship to the following words/ powers – some you will know very well and some you may be meeting for the first time . . .

Herbs, Attitudes and Archetypes of the Celts –

Apple cider vinegar	Airmid, Air
Burdock	Brighid
Comfrey	Common sense, Charms, Courage
Dandelion	Determination, Diancecht
Elecampane	Earth, Energy
Fennel	Fire, Faith, Forgiveness, Fresh air
Garlic	Gratitude
Hawthorn	Honey, Humour, Hygiene
Lavender	Love, Labour, Laughter
Mallow	Meditation, Moderation, Mediation
Nettle	Need
Onion	Opportunity, Optimism
Plaintain	Prayer, Play
Queen Anne's Lace	Quest
Rosehips	Reconnection, Rest
St. John's wort	Simplicity
Thyme	Time
Vervain	Vitality
Weeds	Wonder, Water, Wholeness
Yarrow	You

We of European descent, living on other continents, often feel we have to 'borrow' from other Nature religions and healing traditions in order to deepen our spirituality beyond Judeo-Christian perimeters. In fact, we are the inheritors of ancient rituals, symbols, mythologies, and healing knowledge, a diverse, Earth-loving, life-enriching magico-spiritual system, tens of thousands of years old, oppressed and discriminated against for two thousand years and now beginning to enjoy a blossoming renaissance. This heritage includes rituals and ceremonies to mark, empower and celebrate the cycles and seasons of Earthly life. Our ancestors used plants for healing, beat drums and chanted incantations and danced to commune with Spirit, knew how to live ecologically and harmoniously with Nature, cherished family and community and lived their lives in accordance with the laws and rhythms of Nature.

They knew how to communicate with animals, plants and stones to determine their healing gifts. They considered themselves to be the beloved children of the Divine Mother/Father, with all the creatures of Nature their brothers and sisters. Their magic, their wisdom, their experiences are encoded within the cells of our bodies, in the eternally spiralling DNA memory coursing through our veins. We have only to listen, to remember, to re-root ourselves in our own proud history, thereby creating a strong foundation from which we can build a brighter future and contribute to the Circle of Healing.

Chinese, Ayurvedic and Native American Herbalism have been accorded their place of honour in the recent Herbal Renaissance.

Now it is time for Celtic, European Herbalism and within that sphere, Irish Herbalism, to take its rightful place alongside them.

An ancient knowledge, full of wisdom and common sense, worthy of respect, Celtic Herbalism recognises Nature as manifest Divinity and illness as a disconnection from that Divinity. It recognises the Spirit in all things and works to reconnect that Spirit to its Divine source. It recognises Life as a Web, that each thing has its place on the Web and that what affects the part affects the whole.

In Celtic Herbalism, plants (and trees and rocks and animals and . . .) are recognised as individuals with their own living spirit and must be approached with respect. The plants are the teachers. When the plant Spirits are approached with love and respect, they will harmonise with our needs and give generously of their healing gifts. If they are taken from for the purpose of exploitation, then certainly their gifts will not be as full and may cause uncomfortable side effects. This is not scientific fact, this is primordial law.

A basic example of this is the different effect of on herbal tea compared to a pharmaceutical plant extract – Mother Nature builds protection into the plant token in its whole state. When the biochemical constituent is extracted and administered without its protective wholeness, it can cause discomfort, addiction and other negative side effects. Valerian, when taken as a 'whole plant' tea or tincture, is calming and sedative. Valium, it's pharmaceutical derivative, causes depression, nightmares and becomes addictive.

Plants participate in every phase of Life. They clean and revitalise the Air, they fuel the Fire, they transport the Water, and they feed the Earth and all Her children.

Plants are amazing allies and teachers, enhancing and aiding so many facets of our lives. They grace our world with their beauty, importing vitality and healing for our bodies, minds and hearts, lending themselves to a myriad or crafts, providing shelter, clothing, food and fuel, instrumental to health and happiness, enriching all Life with their own spirit. The Plants are Beings, not things to be exploited.

Gina McGarry

Acknowledgements

Deepest gratitude and infinite appreciation to all those who have helped to bring this book to fruition.

My mum and dad; John and Val Downey, Eileen Lawrence, Gay Brabazon, Kate Marden, Venice Mason, Jane Brideson, Pete Gotto and Chris Render at Green Magic

All my students and clients along the way. My excellent teachers, including Rosemary Gladstar, Starhawk and Susun Weed, Vicki Noble, Hallie Iglehart Austin, James Green, Mindy Green, Amanda McQuade Crawford, David Hoffman, Michael Moore, Tim Blakely

And, of course, Brighid Herself, the light of my life.

Thank you and bless you all.

This publication is intended to provide educational information on the covered subject.It is not intended to take the place of personalised medical counselling, diagnosis and treatment from a trained healthcare professional.

CHAPTER 1

BRIGHID – GODDESS OF HEALING

Many ancient manuscripts, dating from 800 AD, confirm that the practitioners of the healing arts in Ireland were the repositories of knowledge handed down from the oldest professional body in Europe – the herbal physicians. The renowned and impeccable character of the Irish schools of medicine drew students from all over Europe. Since Ireland did not suffer the Roman invasion as in Europe and Britain, and avoided the proscribing of their language and culture (at least until the English got there!), Irish manuscripts offer the preserved wealth of druidical and healing traditions.

The Celtic physicians placed great importance on cleanliness, fresh air and pure water in the treatment of the sick and wounded; simple yet powerful allies of healing. Their houses were built on the banks of streams, with four doors, one in each direction, so that all that happened within could be observed and one door could always be open to allow fresh air in, no matter which way the wind was blowing. Baths, sweat-houses and surgery (including brain) were employed and the manuscripts are full of herbs, prayers, chants and charms to heal many various diseases.

Each area had its own physician who took on apprentices. The apprentice paid a fee to cover their room, board and lessons for the duration of their learning, often travelling great distances, even overseas, to receive instruction. Teaching was by oral instruction and example. Trainees of a particular teacher formed certain spiritual lineages, teaching styles and practical skills, as with Brighid's Aid-women or in Tibet, where Buddhist masters founded particular orders. When the physician went on a house call, the person receiving aid was compelled by Brehon Law to provide food and lodging to physician and apprentice in addition to payment, which was determined according to the seriousness of the disease and the person's ability to pay.

Ancient legends suggest that the Tuatha de Danaan, the children of Dana, Mother Goddess, Great Queen of the Heavens, came from the doomed Atlantis to Ireland.

Great in magic, preceding the emigration of the Celts, it is from them that the Fairie (and many of us) are descended.

From the four great Atlantean cities they came, bringing with them the Four Sacred Tools. From Findias, the city of the East, came Nuada and his people, carrying the Sword of Truth. From the South and the city of Gorias came Lugh, Lord of Light, the Many-skilled One and his people, the keepers of the Spear of Light. Daghda, the Good Father and his people came from the West, the city of Murias, and brought with them the Cauldron of Plenty. Morrigan, the great Queen, brought her people and the Lia Fail, the Stone of Destiny, from the northern city of Failias.

Brighid, daughter of Dana and the Daghda, was also among their number. She was the epitome of Divine Radiance and the uniting force of the Danaan as they settled in their new home. She brought many blessings to share with all the people, including the indigenous Fir Bolg. She brought the gifts of healing, poetry, writing and smithcraft. She infused the hearthfires with Her warmth and light and the springs with Her healing grace. She set up centres all over Eire and trained Her priestesses in the healing arts, that they might serve the people. She governed and assisted the fire of the home's hearth, the poet's heart, the healer's hands and the smith's forge.

Thus, the symbolism of Brighid's Cross. The four arms represent the four cities, the four elements, with Brighid spiralling in the centre.

Brighid is always the unifying force among peoples and the Elements.

In 1996, I was privileged to participate in the Feile Bride (Brighid's Festival) in Kildare, Ireland. It was in this place that Her priestesses kept Brighid's fire for thousands of years and then, with the influx of Christianity, it was kept by Her nuns. In 1220 AD, the Bishop in power at the time ordered it put out for being too 'pagan'.

The people rebelled, however, and it was kept alight for another 300 years, but was finally put out 'for good' in the 1500s. And so it lay dark for over 400 years.

In 1992, two Brigidine Sisters, Mary Minehan and Phil O'Shea, founded Solas Bhride in Kildare and re-established Brighid's Flame, which they have since continually kept in the form of an ever-burning candle. On Brighid's Day, 1996, over 400 years after the Flame had been doused, Sister Mary and Sister Phil, along with the members of

Cairde Bhride, organised an 'official' re-lighting ceremony, beginning at Brighid's Well, about a mile outside of Kildare Town.

At dusk, about 50 people from the local community, all ages, all walks of life, gathered at the Well to honour the Goddess and the Saint. The participants were a mixture of local pagans, Catholics and atheists (for whom Brighid is the Muse) and myself and a traveling companion. Candles, placed along the course of the stream and well, illuminated the night sky. Irish voices spoke softly in the star and candlelight. Sister Mary began the ritual, reminding us all to prepare ourselves before entering the sanctuary,

We gathered before the statue of Brighid. She was so powerfully beautiful with the candles lit all around her and Her waters flowing beneath Her feet. A woman began to sing praise songs for Her and the people joined in. Four youths each lit a candle and invoked blessings for Peace, Justice, Healing and Inspiration. We made our way to the Well at the end of the sanctuary, where Sister Mary invited us to decide what we would like to let go of, to give up to Brighid to be healed. We circled around the well, holding hands with each other, each of us giving up our hurts to be reborn as Hope. Then, 9 torches were lit, representing Her 9 Priestesses, and were handed out. Gay Brabazon, who has since become my dear friend, handed one to me and in that moment, transformed my life. And so, on behalf of all my sisters and brothers in America who also love Her, chanting their names as I walked, I carried a torch for Brighid the mile back to Kildare. Tears of overwhelming joy and gratitude threatened to engulf me, but I focused on this incredible honour and determined to bear the Flame with strength and grace. To her ancient Fire Temple we walked, accompanied by the music of a lone bagpipe. There, after over 400 years of 'dormancy', Brighid's sacred flame was relit.

Since then, Sister Mary has passed 'seed' lights from the perpetual candle to people from all over the world. We have carried this light back to our communities where we, too, keep the perpetual Flame of Brighid, that Her compassion and healing may spread.

QUALITIES OF BRIGHID, GODDESS, SAINT AND MUSE

Brighid is a lady of principle.

She is assertive in an elegant manner.

She knows how to achieve Her goals without alienating Her associates and friends.

3

Above all, Brighid is an idealist who will achieve through dedication and perseverance.

If anyone is a winner, Brighid is.

Brighid is compassionate, caring, loyal, unselfish and feminine. She is strong in insight and intuition. She is fun-loving and can show a tendency towards flirtatious and mischievious acts.

Brighid – 'The High One', 'Strength', 'Exalted One'

Planet – the Sun and the Moon.

Colours – gold, silver, green and blue.

Plants – crocus, primrose, dandelion, blackberry, oak, vervain.

Symbols – cow, sheep, serpent, bell, embroidery tools, fire, milk, springs, the oak tree, rainbows.

Feast Day – 1 February: Imbolc – means 'ewe milk', 'lustration', 'purification'.

Blessed Brighid

Mother of Light
   Accept this incense as a symbol of Breath,
   That we may know it's sacredness.
   Help us to remember that when we breathe in,
   We breathe in your nourishing love.
   And when we breathe out,
   We nourish you with ours.

Blessed Brighid

Mother of the Flame
   Accept this oil as a symbol of Fire.
   That we may know its sacredness.
   Help us to remember that
   The Fire of Your Spirit dances within us
   As the Fire of our Spirits dance within you.

Blessed Brighid

Mother of the Waters
   Accept these fluids as a symbol of them,
   That we may know their sacredness.
   Help us to remember that
   Your healing waters flow through our veins.
   As your heartbeat nourishes us,
   May every beat of our hearts nourish you.

Blessed Brighid

Woman of the Earth
  Accept this food as your symbol,
  That we may know your sacredness.
  Help us to remember
  That from Her body, we are born and nurtured
  As our bodies nourish Her.

Another great physician of the Tuatha de Danaan (Toota day danun) was Diancecht (pronounced 'jyanku). The Celts perceived him as a Druid of phenomenal skill and knowledge, his name meaning 'Vehement Power'. It is said that he recognised 14 disorders of the stomach, for which he prescribed plant remedies. The oldest known recipe is known as 'Diancecht's Porridge', made from hazel buds, dandelion, chickweed and wood sorrel, boiled with oatmeal and taken morning and evening for the relief of colds, sore throats and 'the presence of evil things' in the body. He also prescribed frankincense mixed with white wine to restore the memory and considered saffron to be an excellent tonic. His use of frankincense indicates some kind of trade relationship with Arabia, since it was not indigenous to Ireland!

When the de Danaans arrived in Ireland, they had to do battle with the Fir Bolg, the indigenous people of Eire. The Fir Bolg lived close to the Earth and followed the path of the Moon. They had been oppressed and enslaved by the Fomorii, a northern race of seafarers, and were not inclined to welcome more invaders. And so the first Battle of Moytura was fought in County Sligo in 487 BC.

Diancecht, with his son, Miach, and his daughter, Airmid, assembled a great cauldron, filled with a herbal potion. They chanted healing spells over it and any warrior who was wounded was put into it and restored to life. Any wound could be healed as long as the body remained intact. This was not the case for the de Danaan chieftain, Nuada, however. In the fray, his hand was severed from his body. Diancecht fashioned a hand made of silver and attached it so that it was almost as the hand he had lost. Almost, but not quite. In order to rule, a chieftain had to be perfect, and the de Danaan were most distressed to lose Nuada, whom they greatly loved and respected. Now, Miach, Diancecht's son, had embalmed the severed hand. He chanted spells over it and reattached it to Nuada's arm, making him whole again. The people rejoiced, but Diancecht became so enraged with jealousy that his son had surpassed him in skill that he killed him! When Miach was buried at Tara, a herb grew from each part of his body that would heal that part of the body – dandelion grew from his

5

liver, chamomile from his belly, comfrey from his bones, hawthorn from his heart and so on, 365 in all. Miach's sister, Airmid, came to weep at his grave and, when she saw this, she knew what to do. She gathered the plants into her cloak, keeping them in the proper arrangement and travelled around the countryside, sharing the healing wisdom with the people, thus developing the knowledge of herbs correlating with body systems and organs and becoming the patroness of herbalists.

THE WEB OF LIFE

The world view of many ancient cultures is that of a web, a holistic inter-connection between all things. The Web of Life encompasses and connects

The aspects of our Selves, physical, mental, emotional, spiritual
The community
The aspects of Nature
The aspects of Healing
All things in the Universe

It is the world view that we follow here at Brighid's Academy. This point of view allows multiple possibilities in life and healing, honouring indi-viduality and uniqueness. It takes us out of polarity thinking and offers creative choices. In American culture, when two people disagree, it is assumed that there can be only one right answer, that is, there is an 'either-or' mentality. This creates polarity and the argument can escalate all the way to war. What I have termed a 'both-and' mentality moves us beyond the limited choice of only two possibilities. It allows for a third, fourth, fifth and more possibilities. So rather than the linear argument between doctors and herbalists, where both parties judge and resist each other ('My way is right! No, my way is right!), we could take the 'both-and', multiple-choice philosophy (you have knowledge and I have knowledge) then we can work together to provide healing for the individual. The web is a powerful tool when seeking understanding of a thing, whether it is the web of our astrological chart or the interconnec-tion between animals and plants or ...

When one thing is affected on the web, then everything else is, too, for good or ill. As healers, we are the spider, the mender of the web. We gain skill in sitting with someone and being able to determine or perceive where the web has broken down and then we can help them to reconnect the strands of their being.

Contemplate a web – see it as a representation of all the aforesaid aspects. This is the ancient shamanic way of all indigenous peoples, including our Celtic and pre-Celtic ancestors, which allowed them to live in relative peace and prosperity for thousands and thousands of years, until linear consciousness took over. We are not separate from Nature – we are of Nature. All things have their equal, yet different, place on the web.

HISTORICAL METHODS OF HEALING
(with thanks to Susun Weed)

There are many approaches to healing. History proves the longevity, balance, effectiveness and affordability of the path of the traditional healer. Contemplate the following ages, seek to understand which beliefs have affected your reality and strive to make whatever changes you deem appropriate for yourself.

Scientific – 1500 AD to present

Attitude, belief and projection

Disease and death are the enemy to be vanquished at all costs (to the
    environment, the patient's bank balance, and even their lives).
The war on cancer, aids, drugs, etc. the magic bullet = kill the disease.
The body is the machine, the healer the mechanic.
Take the non-working part out; replace it with a 'new one'.
Power is placed on drugs and surgery, diagnostic machines.
The patient says, 'Fix me'.

Remedies

Measurable repetition, precise, odourless, tasteless, costly. Vulnerable to interactions with other drugs, food, environmental factors.

Heroic – 1000 BC to present

Attitude, belief and projection

Disease and death are the result of toxins, in the air, the food, the water, etc.
    We have 'dirtied' the temple and must cleanse/punish ourselves – purge, purge, punish, punish. No wonder bulimia is such an issue.
    The healer as saviour, 'Trust me, I will heal you'.

Stimulants, purges, enaemas, effectors – herbs like senna, wormwood, herbs that push the body to do something – often with side effects.

Remedies

Complex, difficult, scarce, exotic, expensive.

Shamanic or Wise Woman Way – 50000 BC (probably millennia before) to present

Attitude, belief and projection

Disease is a message from Spirit and an opportunity for change.

It is a perfect manifestation of complete being.

The Self as healer, the 'healer' as midwife, You are giving birth to a new you and the healer serves as the midwife of that process.

The ancient ways gave as much honour to the mundane as they did the miraculous.

The 'shamanic' way is about living in harmonious relationship with Nature, availing ourselves of all the allies therein – the plants, the animals, the sky, the sea, the earth, the wind, the fire, the water, the soil and on and on . . . .

To 'shamanically' heal, one must take on the attitude of a warrior, a warrior for Truth, who faces challenge, willing to do what is right, rather than what is comfortable.

Shamanic discipline is about getting in shape, physically, mentally, emotionally and spiritually.

In the shamanic traditions, health is more than the absence of physical suffering. It is an exuberance and a feeling of vitality and passion for Life. Illness is one of Nature's teachers, an opportunity for change. When we are ill, we are being called to undertake a journey into the Underworld to meet with our shadow and learn something. The Spirit of Healing works in union with Nature, always adaptable, changeable, limitless.

'Trust yourself'. Your body is miraculous in its healing ability and if you simply give it nourishment and encouragement, it can very often heal itself.

The Wise Woman Way is based on unconditional love, nourishment and integration. Remedies are common, invisible, local, familiar, messy, fun, simple, easy, bioregional weeds, free, cheap, trace minerals.

Nourish the cells – they are constantly growing and dying, therefore we are constantly renewing cell by cell, every minute of every day. The liver is replaced, cell by cell, every six weeks, the kidneys once a month, the blood every three weeks.

So, having contemplated the three major modalities or styles of healing, which approach do you most respond to? Remember that we do not have to deny or diminish any other philosophy. Remember to remain flexible and inclusive – true healing is never exclusive of any modality that will bring it about. If, for example, one of my loved ones was in a car accident, I would acknowledge my limitations in the situation and allow the 'heroic' doctors of the emergency room to save their life and restore homoeostasis (physiological stability) and then I would use my herbs and other healing modalities to aid them in their recovery. If someone chooses chemotherapy or surgery to treat their cancer, I would honour that choice and work with them to keep their strength and nourishment levels up and minimise the toxicity of their chosen treatment. I look forward to the day when all modalities can work together in mutual cooperation and respect, with the healing of the individual the goal, rather than fighting over who's right or who's best.

LEARNING TO COMMUNICATE WITH THE PLANTS

Practice acute observation with an open, exploring mind. Allow yourself to become fully conscious, fully present and fully alive

There are many different ways to 'read' the plants' messages to us. First and foremost, they communicate to us through our senses, through sight, smell, sound, taste and touch. Engaging the five physical senses opens the sixth, intuitive sense. So when you approach a plant to make its acquaintance, introduce yourself and then look at it from the point of view of the bee or the ant. Get up close and examine the colour, shape, texture and veinings of the leaves, stems and flowers. Then look at it from the point of view of a bird hovering above it – what is its environment, what does it grow with, does it spread out or remain compact, is it growing in sun or shade? Then, asking permission, take a bit of the leaf and smell, touch and taste it. Is it sweet, spicy, sour, fuzzy, smooth, etc.? All these things will tell you something about the plant's personality and, every time you go back to the plant, she will tell you something else about herself. From here on, I will refer to the plants as 'she'. The feminine gender includes the masculine within it (both-and) and this allows me to relate to them as my foster children, sister, brother, elder, etc. Always ask permission when harvesting and realise that, to the plant beings, you are a God/dess, you are omnipotent, you have the power of life and death over them. When the plants come to know you as a being of integrity, as someone who seeks to contribute to harmony and balance, they will happily cooperate with you, giving freely of their medicines. Many of them, like us, are destined to be healers, and we help each other to fulfil that destiny. Many of them are warriors, willing to sacrifice their lives to contribute to the Great Harmony. They do not fear death, understanding that all life feeds on death and that the spirit is immortal. There can be no life without death. The issue is whether or not that death is given consciously and with deep gratitude or it is given unconsciously for purposes of exploitation.

Establish a relationship with one or two plants at a time, engaging with them in as many ways as possible for a week at a time. Look at them, taste them, smell them, bathe and sleep with them, take them into your body as tea, sleep with them, read about them . . . When growing plants in your garden, realise that we are accepting responsibility to be 'foster mothers' to some of Mother Earth's children. If you're like me, you'll fret over them and rejoice over them and have to keep them out of each other's 'rooms'. Don't coddle them too much or they won't become strong and adaptable. The 'wilder' the plants are, the stronger their medicine.

When gathering plants from the wild, never take more than 10–20%, always leave a gift in exchange for theirs and leave the place better than you found it. Appropriate and traditional gifts are Moon blood, bread, water, wine, honey, a song. Record your observations and experiences. Don't be afraid to make mistakes – the plants are unconditionally loving and incredibly forgiving (there are exceptions, of course – Mother Nettle will bite if she is not approached very carefully, with respect!)

Timing

Gather nourishing, tonifying plants during the waxing Moon in a water or earth sign.

Gather plants that will 'reduce' things in the body (bacteria, inflammation, growths and tumours) during the waning Moon in a water or earth sign.

Use the air and fire times to clean, clear, study.

Gather roots either in the early spring before the top growth begins or in the autumn after the top growth has died back. Chop and spread on screens or baskets to dry.

Gather seeds in the autumn. Place in paper bags with holes for ventilation.

Gather leaves and stems (aerial parts) up to and including the time that they flower. Remove any browned or damaged bits and either hang in bunches or spread on screens to dry. (Following the lunar guidelines ensures that they grow back quickly, sometimes offering two, three, four harvests during the season.)

THE DOCTRINE OF SIGNATURES

A plant will often resemble the disease, organ or personality for which it is the remedy. It is important to engage our intuition, our imagination and our common sense if we are to accurately use this process. Confirm your findings with knowledgeable backup (books, other herbalists, etc.) These are general guidelines with all kinds of exceptions, so stay loose and flexible. Remember that plants are as diverse and unpredictable as human beings and some of them are real tricksters! Work with the plants in external ways until you're sure they're not poisonous. Just because we can't take a plant internally doesn't mean it doesn't have healing gifts. Foxglove is very poisonous taken internally, but I gather the fallen blossoms, dry them and add them to incense blends to heighten connection with the Fairie folk.

PLANT IDENTIFICATION – TASTE

There are six flavours.

Bitter

This is probably the most important to health and vitality and the least experienced taste in our culture. The 'American' diet is more sweet and salty. The physiological action of bitter on the tongue triggers the liver to open and cool, stimulates digestive juices and hormonal secretion, tonifies (strengthens) the digestive and endocrine systems, supports assimilation and hormonal balance and aids fat digestion. Bitter sends energy downwards and helps with grounding. It is rare that I don't put a bitter in a formula.

Many plants are bitter, such as dandelion, dock, horehound and mugwort, becoming the most bitter when they flower. This is why, so many times, we harvest herbs when in flower, to gather the strongest bitter quality. Roots of plants are the most bitter in the spring and autumn, increasing in sweetness after the first frost. People will react strongly, often with repulsion (there's an old saying, 'The stronger they react, the more they need it'), but will find it tastes better as their body adjusts, realising the benefits.

Examples: Dandelion (mild), dock (strong), wormwood (strongest), horehound, Oregon grape, hops (at least when people drink beer, they're getting some bitter!), and so many others.

Take your tastebuds out to an organic garden or wildplace and see how many you can identify . . . remember that a little goes a long way with this taste.

Sweet

In its natural, unrefined, state, sweet is nourishing and warming to the body and the soul, explaining why we reach for the chocolate when life doesn't seem so good. Sweet is helpful in degenerative diseases, benefiting hormonal balance, nerves and muscles, the digestive system and the pancreas, supporting deep and effective nourishment.

Too much sweet in the blood can encourage heat and many different infections. 'Moderation in all things, everything in balance'.

Examples: Fruits, rice, squash, winter roots, ginseng, burdock, dandelion flowers, fennel, licorice, stevia.

Sour

Sour helps to stimulate digestion and causes contraction which, on the positive side, strengthens muscle and organ tissues, while overdoing it can debilitate and weaken.

Sour can indicate the presence of oxalic acid which, in large quantities, can cause aching in joints. Combining with sweet offers balance and protection, e.g. apple cider vinegar and honey.

Examples: Sorrel, miner's lettuce, cranberries, spinach, lemon.

Astringent

The action of astringent is tightening and toning to body tissue. Too much astringency, without the balance of demulcents, can be overly drying, causing constipation and stiff joints. The experience on the tongue feels cool and drying.

Examples: Blackberry, raspberry, nettles, sage (really, really astringent!).

Acrid or spicy

What is life without a little spice? Spice warms the blood, bringing it to the surface, warming our skin, while allowing the internal organs to cool. Stimulating to metabolism, libido and the circulatory system, it breaks up stagnancy, and decongests, tonifies the mucous membranes, brings blood flow to the digestive system. Spice acts as a catalyst for the other herbs in the remedy and aids absorption.

Examples: Ginger, cinnamon, basil, marjoram, hot peppers, peppergrass, vitex, angelica mustard, horseradish.

Salt

Salt affects the moisture balance of the body, maintaining moisture with a small amount, causing dehydration in large amounts. Too much salt can throw off electrolyte balance, put strain on the heart, lungs and kidneys, overstimulate the nervous system and endocrine glands and cause cellular dysfunction.

Examples: Sea vegetables, celery, chickweed, Queen Anne's Lace.

PLANT IDENTIFICATION: COLOUR

There is an exception to every rule, but the colour of the flower/fruit will often indicate which part of the body/psyche the plant will have affinity for.

Red

Root centre – survivability, connection to the Earth and ancestors.

Energizing, stimulating, heating. Encourages good circulation and strengthens blood.

Breaks up and moves stagnant, sluggish conditions.

Conditions: Anaemia, colds, constipation, paralysis, listlessness, physical debility.

Plants (can also include pink) red rose, rosehips, red raspberry, red apples, St. John's wort (think of the extract colour) mallows, red clover, wild ginger.

Exception: Red opium poppy.

Orange

Second centre – creativity, sexuality, fertility.

Warming, cheering, strengthens the will, courage, aids mental and physical assimilation, encourages optimum reception of nourishment.

Conditions: Sexual dysfunction, impotence, infertility, incontinence, colitis, rheumatism.

Plants: Calendula, nasturtium, pumpkin, sweet potatoes.

Yellow

Solar plexus – self-esteem, ability to take action.

Inspiring, awakening, nourishes confidence and trust, strengthens the digestive system, including the liver and pancreas, also the kidneys and adrenal glands.

Conditions: Depression, diabetes, indigestion, adrenal exhaustion, menopause, liver troubles.

Plants: Yellow flowers/fruits can indicate the presence of flavanoids. Wild mustard, dandelion, St. John's wort, elecampane, lemon, fennel, chamomile.

Exception: Mullein.

Green

The heart – healing, growth and renewal, love, harmony and peace.

Antimicrobial, antiseptic, disinfectant, cooling, calming, soothing. Emotional stabilizer, lowers blood pressure, governs the thymus gland, the cardiovascular system and the lungs.

Conditions: Exhaustion, irritability, heart troubles, inflamed conditions, i.e. rashes, ulcers, bronchitis, immune issues.

Plants: Mugwort, marjoram, nettles, hops. The green plants heal the heart.

Blue

The centre of communication, truth, devotion, sincerity.

Soothing, calming, cooling, febrifuge, anodyne, governs the thyroid, upper respiratory system, nose, throat and mouth.

Conditions: Inflammations, burns, laryngitis, allergies/asthma, mouth infections, thyroid imbalance (metabolism dysfunction, sluggish digestion, dry, coarse skin and hair, heart palpitations, lethargy/depression, poor memory/concentration).

Plants: Comfrey, cornflower, sage, sweet violet, chicory.

Indigo

The Third Eye – intuition, psychic and intellectual abilities, sight, sound, smell, experience.

Deepening, mentally purifying, synergises mental, physical and spiritual bodies; governs the pituitary, nervous system and brain, eyes and ears.

Conditions: Learning disabilities, headaches (migraine), neurological disturbances, brain tumours, stroke.

Plants: Heartsease.

Violet

Connection to Spirit, the Cosmos. Purifying, calming and centring. Values, consciousness, faith. Inspires highest ideals.

Conditions: Energetic disorders, spiritual depression, extreme sensitivity to light and sound, insomnia, disturbed dreamstate, chronic fatigue not connected to any physical disorder.

Plants: Lavender, skullcap, rosemary, violet.

REQUIRED SUPPLIES FOR HERBAL PREPARATIONS

Herbs – fresh and dry
Menstruums – vodka – 6 gallons
Apple cider vinegar – 2 gallons
Glycerine (optional)
Raw honey – 1 lb.
Oils – olive oil – $\frac{1}{2}$ gallon
Almond or apricot kernel oil – 8 oz.
Essential oils – lavender (*Lavendula off.* or augustifolia)
Lemon
Thyme (*Thymus vulgaris*)

Plus your personal choices or those required for recipes

Wide-mouthed jars – varying sizes up to 1 quart. You will need enough to store your dry herbs and make tinctures in.
Bottles – 1 oz. to 16 oz. Coloured bottles are ideal to protect your preparations from light, otherwise be sure to store in darkness.
A sturdy mortar and pestle
An incense pot
Incense charcoal
100% cotton muslin cloth – 2 yards
Assorted white linen cloths
An assortment of bowls – small, medium and large
Two non-aluminium cooking pots – 1 pint and 1 quart

Wooden spoons and chopsticks
A good knife and cutting board
Measuring cup
Flat baskets and racks for drying
An assortment of funnels
An assortment of labels

TEXTBOOKS

A Modern Herbal, Mrs. M. Grieve, Dover Publications, Inc. 1971.
Know Your Body – The Atlas of Anatomy, Trevor Weston, M.D. Ulysses
      Press.
The Master Book of Herbalism, Beyerl, Paul Phoenix Publishing Inc., 1984.
Peterson's Field Guides – Eastern/Central Medicinal Plants, Foster/Duke
      Houghton Mifflin Co.

CELTIC LUNAR ASTROLOGY

Our most ancient ancestors followed the Moon before they followed
the Sun. The Moon in our natal chart represents our heart and the
way we individually experience our emotions and feelings, what each
of us needs in order to feel secure and nourished and safe. It governs
our daily habits, patterns and activities, travelling through each sign
every two to three days. We set our emotional tone for the month
when the Moon is in the same sign as our personal Moon, so make
sure you're in a good mood! Since ancient times, plant growers have
practised the wisdom of gardening according to certain lunar phases. I
recommend obtaining a good lunar calender (Llewellyn puts out a
pocket-sized one) and keep a journal of your own moods and experiences during each sign. Everyone tends to feel better in some phases
than others. This will help determine your own relationship with
signs and phases and help you plan life activities more appropriately. I
have found this wisdom to be a most empowering tool, both personally
and in my healing work. In the garden, it has helped me grow strong
healthy plants, even in adverse conditions. When I know the Moon
sign of my clients, I can get to the 'heart' of the matter more quickly.
It helps me to know when it is best to act and when it is best to be
still.

Moon in Aries – Cardinal Fire, Mars, 1st House

Energy tendencies

Enthusiasm, ambition, energetic, activity, initiation, new beginnings, changes, spontaneity.

Irritated, competitive, overly-assertive, impulsive, narrow or single minded.

Carries themes forward that were dreamed of in Pisces.

The sprout, pushing up toward the light.

The newborn, desiring to express itself.

Adventure, rather than security.

Events occur rapidly and pass rapidly.

Physical body – tempers, head injuries

The head, skull, sinuses and jaw.

Animal allies

The ewe and the ram.

Plants

Blackberry, wild mustard. Plants with stingers, thorns, thistles. Plants that spread through runners can have an 'Arien' flavour. Warrior plants that grow where Mother Earth has been disturbed – the way black-berry grows where the ground has been dug for waterpipes, for example.
Warming.

Deities/archtypes

Scotia, the Warrior Goddess. Banba, Irish Amazon. Cuchaillean, the Ulster Hero.

Moon in Taurus – Fixed Earth, Venus, 2nd House

A time of

Security, simplicity, sensuality.

Conservative, mellow, yet stubborn.

Grounded, practical, physical demonstration.

Money and business concerns.

Things begun now last longest and tend to increase in value.

Appreciation of earthly beauty and the arts.

Maintains what was initiated in Aries.

Food, gardening, Nature, banking.
Beautifying the environment.

Throat ailments: the physical body

The neck, throat, tonsils, thyroid.

Animal allies

The cow and bull.

Plants

Rose, prunella. Plants with mucilagenous, beautiful flowers, pleasant smells.

Fruits

In the garden/pharmacy – along with Cancer, the very best time for planting and harvesting. Herbs planted now will have strong root systems and lush growth. A good time to feed the soil, make medicines, especially nutrient, strengthening ones.

Deities

Boann, the Cow Goddess. Eire, Tara, Goddesses of the Land. Dagda, the Good Father.

Moon in Gemini – Mutable Air, Mercury, 3rd House

Energy tendencies

Lively, quick-witted, social.
Intellectual brainstorming.
Studying, teaching, speaking, thinking, talking, communicating.
Inconsistent, fickle – things begun now are easily affected by outside influences.
The curious child who wants all the answers holds sway – bores easily, restless.
Duality – ability to see both sides.
Creative communication.

The physical body

Lungs, arms, hands, nervous system.

Animal ally

The bee.

Plants

Wood betony, lavender. Plants with fine divided leaves and stems (the twins of Gemini). Plants with subtle odours.

In the garden/pharmacy – good time for pest removal, weed removal. Study and research. Make incenses and other potions of air.

Deities/archtypes

Bloeddwedd, the Flower Maiden.

Moon in Cancer – Cardinal Water, Moon, 4th House

A time of

Emotional, nurturing, growth.
Homelife and family ties.
Reflection on the past, nostalgia, sentimental.
Emotional rapport between people.
Avoid hurting others and being hurt.
Tendency to overeat, 'smother' with love.
Discomfort in unfamiliar surroundings.
Planting, collecting, harvesting, healing.

The physical body

Breasts, stomach, womb, liver.

Animal ally

The crab.

Plants

Motherwort, marshmallow. Plants with lots of moisture. Soft, juicy leaves. White flowers, fruit.

In the garden/pharmacy – the ultimate time to plant and harvest. The healing energy is strongest in plants gathered at this time and will grow back even more abundantly. Herbs planted now will use water most efficiently and can adapt to drought conditions. Hair cut during this cycle will grow faster.

Deities/archtypes

Danu, the Universal Mother. Brighid, Goddess of Compassion and Healing. Dagda, the Good Father: in this aspect, Keeper of the Cauldron of Plenty.

Moon in Leo – Fixed Fire, Sun, 5th House

A time of

Openness, warmth, outgoing, social, generous.
Prideful, high drama, sensitive egos.
Need for attention.
Parties, entertaining, performing.
Emphasis on self, central ideas or institutions, away from connection with
    others.
Romance, affection, recognition, admiration, ambition, creativity.
Working with children, fun and games.

The physical body

Heart, upper back, spine.

Animal allies

The lion, cats.

Plants

Dandelion, daisy. Look like the Sun. Improve circulation.
    In the garden – good time for weeding, making oils, having a garden
party!

Deities/archtypes

Grainne, the Sun Goddess. Maeve, the Warrior Queen. Lugh, the Sun
King. Finn McCool, the fair Warrior.

Moon in Virgo – Mutable Earth, Mercury, 6th house

A time of

Details, methodical work, organising and finishing.
Physical sensitivity, self-improvement.
Analytical, thinking, considering, figuring.
Intellectual pursuits.
Concern for health and food.
Community service.
House cleaning, gardening.
Very sensitive to criticism.

The Physical Body

Pancreas, small intestine, spleen, liver.

Animal allies

The field mouse.

Plants

Queen Anne's Lace, corn, grains, vines. Plants that stimulate the digestive tract.

In the garden – excellent for all planting activities, especially food and field plants. Attend to detail work, e.g. fixing the fence, getting that rock border just right, etc.

Deities/archtypes

Cernal, the Harvest Maiden. The Grain God.

Moon in Libra – Cardinal Air, Venus, 7th House

A time of

Art, beauty, romance, relationships.
Meditation, cooperation, harmony, refinement, elegance.
'We' oriented – least egocentric.
Increased self-awareness, interaction with others.
Teamwork and partnerships.
Social gatherings, intellectual stimuli.

The physical body

The lower back, kidneys and bladder.

Plants

Roses, chickweed. Twin pairs of leaves and flowers. Flowers of all kinds.

In the garden/pharmacy – gathering and planting flowers, adding garden art, making flower essences and herbal cosmetics, perfumery.

Deities/archtypes

Edain, the Venus of the Celts. Aongus McOg, the God of Love.

Moon in Scorpio – Fixed Water, Pluto, 8th House

A time of

Solitude, healing, rethinking, integrating.
Insights, research, sexuality, resurrection.

Power plays, manipulation, jealousy.
Passionate, persistent, proud.
Increased psychic power.
Ending of connections.
Moodiness, secretiveness, intensity.
Avoid sarcasm and operations.
Go to the deepest depths.
Transformation and transmutation.
Competitive, obsessive.

The physical body

Reproductive organs, the colon.

Animal allies

The Phoenix, the eagle, the serpent.

Plants

Nettle, poppy. Plants found in remote, shady places. Mind-altering plants. Deep red to black flowers.

In the garden/pharmacy – Best extraction time for 'hard' parts of plants, e.g. resins, tough roots, hard berries, without having to use grain alcohol. The most powerful time for deep, transformational magic.

Deities/archtypes

The Morrigan, Diancecht.

Moon in Sagittarius – Mutable Fire, Jupiter, 9th House

Energy tendencies

Upbeat, optimistic, lively, expansive.
Philosophical, searching for answers.
Humour, high energy, travel, education.
Time for taking risks and expanding.
Confidence, luck.
Everything flows into place if you let it.
Expansionary flights of imagination.
Restlessness, need for adventure and freedom.
Generosity, spontaneity, intuitiveness.

Overspending, overeating, overdoing.
Write for publication, teach, lecture.

The physical body

Thighs, sciatic nerve, hips.

Animal ally

The horse.

Plants

St. John's wort, horsetail. Fiery flowers, expansive growth habits.
    In the garden – weed, clear, expand beds. Make oils and 'fire' potions.

Deities/archtypes

Epona, Macha.

Moon in Capricorn – Cardinal Earth, Saturn, 10th House

Energy tendencies

Sober, serious, cautious, grounded, practical.
Self-discipline, hard work, long-range strategy planning, duty.
Structure, time, history and tradition.
Controlled and institutional activities are favoured.
Energy may be sluggish, use diligence.
Self-determination, new goals, detailed work.
Avoid pessimism and negative outlooks.

The physical body

Knees, bones, teeth, skin.

Animal allies

The goat, the whale.

Plants

Fir, oak, comfrey. Plants with very strong structures, white roots. Few
flowers. Plants that grow in rock.

Deities/archtypes

Cailleagh, the Crone. Cerridwen, Keeper of the Cauldron of Wisdom.
Merlin, the Wise Council.

Moon in Aquarius – Fixed Air, Uranus, 11th House

Energy tendencies

Friendly, outgoing, exchanging.
Trendy, visionary, radical, revolutionary.
Controversial, offbeat, electric.
A need for space, desire for freedom, the unconventional.
A time to express personal uniqueness.
Interest in others based on intellect, not emotions.

The physical body

The ankles, circulatory system, electrical forces in the body, nerves in the spinal column.

Animal ally

The spider.

Plants

Rosemary, St. John's wort. Plants that increase energy.
   In the garden/pharmacy – weed removal, pest removal. Make potions for changing the status quo.

Deities/archtypes

Arianrhod, the Web Weaver.

Moon in Pisces – Mutable Water, Neptune, 12th House

Energy tendencies

Spacey, dreamy, a time of overindulgence.
Not good for making decisions or for clear thinking.
Good for creativity, music, inspiration, the arts, meditation, dreams and
      visions.
Emotional, sentimental, concerned, empathetic.
Spiritual nurturing.
Energy is withdrawn from the surface of Life.
Strong imagination and psychic abilities.
Impressionable, vulnerable, indecisive.
A gentle time.

The physical body

Lymph, immunity, the feet.

Animal allies

Fish, the dolphin, the salmon.

Plants

Wild lettuce, mugwort, skullcap. Plants that induce dreams and visions. Sedatives.

In the garden/pharmacy – good time for planting and harvesting. Excellent for flower essences and other 'ethereal' medicines. Potions that nourish the spirit.

Deities/archtypes

Mananaan MacLir, Lord of the Sea. Selkies, Merpeople.

HERBAL ACTIONS AND ALLIES

Alteratives

Cleansing and building to the blood; important for elimination, especially the skin.

Cleavers (*Galium aperine*), burdock (*Arctium lappa*), Oregon grape (*Mahonia* spp.), nettles (*Urtica dioica*), calendula (*Calendula off.*), Elecampane (*Inula helenium*), dock (*Rumex* spp.), St. John's wort (*Hypericum perforatum*), thyme (*Thymus vulgaris*), chickweed (*Stellaria media*), yarrow (*Achillea millefolium*).

Analgesics

For pain relief.

Valerian (*Valeriana* spp.), crampbark (*Viburnum opulus*), wild lettuce (*Lactuca* spp.), passion flower (*Passiflora* spp.), feverfew (*Tanacetum* spp.), skullcap (*Scutellaria laterifolia*), lavender (*Lavendula off., L. augustifolia*), peppermint (*Mentha piperetum*), chamomile (*Matricarium, Anthemis* spp.).

Anti-catarrhals

Dissolve and clear mucus.

Sage (*Salvia off.*), nettles (*Urtica dioica*), elecampane (*Inula helenium*), mullein (*Verbascum thapsus*), coltsfoot (*Tussilago farfara*), mallow (*Malvia*) fennel (*Foeniculum vulgaris*).

Anti-depressants

Uplifting and soothing to the emotional body.

Borage (*Boragio off.*), vervain (*Verbena off.*), lemon balm (*Melissa off.*), damiana (*Turnera aphrodesiaca*), clary sage (*Salvia sclarea*), St. John's wort (*Hypericum perforatum*).

Anti-microbials

Nature's 'antibiotics' (anti-biotic means 'anti-life', hence the preferred use of anti-microbial). The advantage of herbal anti-microbials is that they deal with the infectious microbes without killing off beneficial flora, etc.

Thyme (*Thymus vulgaris*), sage (*Salvia off.*), rosemary (*Rosmarinus off.*), basil (*Basillica* spp.), marjoram (*Oreganum marjorana*), garlic (*Allium sativum*), onion (*Allium cepa*), (the aforementioned group of herbs affectionately known as 'spaghetti herbs'), yarrow (*Achillum millefolium*), Oregon grape (*Mahonia* spp.), echinecea (*Echinecea augustifolia, purperea*), myrrh (*Comniphora myrrha*).

Anti-spasmodics

To relieve cramps and muscle aches.

Crampbark (*Viburnum opulus*), valerian (*Valeriana* spp.), agrimony (*Agrimonia eupatorium*), chamomile (*Matricaria* and *anthemis* spp.), thyme (*Thymus vulgaris*), marjoram (*Oreganum marjorana*), wild lettuce (*Lactuca* spp.).

Aperients/laxatives

To relieve pelvic congestion and constipation.

Dandelion root (*Taraxacum off.*), dock (*Rumex* spp.), psyllium seed chamomile.

Astringents – to strengthen and tone tissue, curtail flooding and discharge

Yarrow (*Achilleum millefolium*), raspberry/blackberry leaf (*Rubus* spp.), wild geranium (*Geranium* spp.), lady's mantle (*Alchemilla* spp.), wild strawberry (*Fragaria vesca*), shepherd's purse (*Capsella bursa-pastoris*), sage (*Salvia off.*).

Bitters

Aid digestive health, hormonal function, increase energy and help to alleviate depression.

Chamomile, dandelion, dock, yarrow, mugwort, horehound, blessed thistle, Oregon grape.

Carminatives

To dispel gas.

Chamomile, fennel (*Foeniculum vulgare*), dill (*Anethum graveolens*), 'spaghetti herbs'.

Digestive tonics

To prevent heartburn, flatulence, constipation, aid appetite and ensure good assimilation.

Thyme, fennel, dill, dandelion nettles, horehound, 'spaghetti herbs' and water.

Diuretics

Increase urine output and correct water retention.

Dandelion leaf, yarrow, parsley, celery seed, corn, silk.

Diaphoretics

Open the pores and allow elimination through the skin; help to manage fever.

Yarrow, elder flowers (*Sambucus nigra*).

Cardiac tonics

Strengthen cardiac muscle tone, increasing stability and stamina.

Hawthorn (*Crataegus* spp.), motherwort (*Cardiaca leonurus*), rose, geranium essential oil, ylang ylang essential oil, borage (*Boragio off.*).

Hepatics

Strengthen and tone liver function.

Dandelion milk, thistle, yarrow, horehound, burdock, bitters!

Hormonal balancers

Provide the components for individual requirements.

Vitex (*Vitex agnus-castus*), sage (*Salvia off.*), motherwort, red clover (*Trifolium pratense*), bitters.

Immune tonics

To build and strengthen immunity.

Thyme, St John's Wort, usnea, Oregon grape, 'spaghetti herbs'.

Nervine relaxants

Soothe irritability, anxiety, nervousness.

Chamomile, hops (*Humulus lupulus*), motherwort, lemon balm, scullcap (*Scutellaria laterifolia*), hyssop (*Hyssopus off.*), agrimony, sage, basil, marjoram, lavender.

Nutrient herbs

Provide trace minerals and vitamins.

Nettles, comfrey leaf, rosehips, dandelion (whole plant), oatstraw, elecampane, blackberry leaf.

WEAVING THE WEB

To gain the most from the gathered knowledge of this book, you may want to implement the suggestions listed below and at the end of subsequent chapters.

Gather your supplies and books. Set aside some shelf space for your herbal preparations, with an area for those in process and those that are ready to be used.

Take a walk. Look for dandelion and blackberry. Introduce yourself.

Assuming it's a non-polluted area, ask permission to gather some of the plants for healing and then do so. Leave a gift in thanks.

Make tea from these plants, drink it and add it to your bath, sleep with bits of them under your pillow, dry some and burn as incense, return to their habitat and meditate and acutely observe yourself and everything around you. Take notes.

Study the actions and get someone to test you on them. These are a big part of herbal and medical language. It is important to know them!

Begin to incorporate vervain into your daily life as incense, blessing water, in your ritual bath, etc. and experience the deepening of the sense of the sacred.

Study the Celtic lunar astrology, begin a lunar journal and record your moods daily, making note of the sign the Moon and any external observations.

Taste! Give yourself the experience of the six different taste experiences and observe your body's reactions to them (especially bitter!). Record your experiences. What are your favourites? Which ones are you resistant to? Work to establish a balanced, open relation to each and especially to embrace the taste of bitter – you will do great things for your health!

Look! Give yourself the experience of gazing on each of the colours – record your reactions. Again, which are your favourites? Which, if any, are you resistant to?

CHAPTER 2

LADY OF AIR

THE ATTRIBUTES OF BRIGHID

Not only is Brighid a Triple Goddess but She is also the Lady of the Four Elements of Air, Fire, Water, and Earth.

As Lady of Air, she is born at dawn, a column of fire blazes from her head to the sky, signalling the birth of the Holy One.

She is the Patroness of Children, watching over them as the Shepherdess watches over her sheep.

In ancient tradition, She is the Daughter of Danu, Great Universal Mother, and Dagda, the Good Father.

As St. Brigid, She was the daughter of Dubthach, son of Demre, son of Bresal of the sept of Echaid Find Fuathenairt, and the bondwoman Broisech, daughter of Dallbronach of Dal Conchobair in the south of Bregia.

In both traditions, She was given in fosterage to a Druid and endowed with all Knowledge of the Mysteries and Magic.

From the time She was a child, Brigid was prone to giving away Her father's wealth to the poor. In her honour, children in Ireland celebrate Her Feast Day by crafting Bride's Crosses and offering them from house to house, bringing Brigid's blessings. They are always invited in and given food to share with those less fortunate.

The Bride's Cross is then hung over the door of the house. Her light of protection and blessing shines everywhere within, and all around, the home.

She is the guide and companion of students, evident here in a story from the Book of Lismore, an Irish manuscript from the eighth century, author anonymous:

*Brighid was once with Her sheep on the Curragh and she
saw running past her a son of Learning. Nindid the scholar
was he. 'What makes thee run so, O son of Learning,'
Brigid said, 'and what seekest thou?'*

'O Brighid,' said the scholar, 'I am going to Heaven.'

*'Happy is he that goes on that journey,' said Brighid. 'Sit
and say a prayer with me that it may be easy for me to go.'*

*'O Brighid,' said the scholar, 'I have no time, for the
Gates of Heaven are open now, and I fear that they may be
shut against me. Pray that it may be easy for me to go to
Heaven and I will pray that it may be easy for thee and that
thou mayest bring many thousands with thee.'*

*Brighid recited a prayer with him, and he was at peace
thenceforward.*

*And so it came to pass that the patronage of the world's
sons and daughters of learning is with Brighid. And she made
the writing symbols so that words could be heard with the
eyes, even in faraway places.*

In the darkness of winter, She comes to give us hope. She breathes her
warm mist breath upon the land and the crocus appear, reminding us
that spring is coming once again. While there may be cold days still to
come, we know that their end is near and there are warm, bright days
ahead.

For millennia, Brighid was the residing Spirit of an academy of
learning at Her sacred site in Kildare. Young women from families rich
and poor, near and far, came to receive Her teachings and become aid-
women, serving in Her name. Their functions included the preservation
of the traditional sciences, healing remedies, and the laws of the land.
Village women brought them food and, in exchange, the Bride
women taught them how to use the herbs as medicine. The head of the
academy was considered to be the physical incarnation of the Goddess
and, when elected, took the name Brighid.

Feille Bhride, the Festival of Bride, announces a joyous time of purification and renewal and hope. It is the first breath of spring and the ewe's
milk (Imbolc) flows again, offering fresh nourishment to the people after
the winter's dried provisions. On this day, She breathes new life into the
world, spreading Her green cloak across the land.

Aid-women laid blue cloth on the Earth to absorb the healing mist
formed by Her sacred breath, using them to cool fevered brows and
burns and rashes. They open the doors of their homes at dawn and

welcome Brighid in:

> *Bhride! Solas geal!*
> *Gabh isteach!*
> *Gabh isteach!*
> *Caed mile failte!*

> *Brighid! Bright light!*
> *Come in!*
> *Come in!*
> *One hundred thousand welcomes!*

> *Today is the day of Bride*
> *The serpent shall come from the mound*
> *I will not molest the serpent*
> *Nor will the serpent molest me.*

As the patroness and muse of poets and writers, teachers and musicians, She blesses us with inspiration, imagination, words, melodies and memory. She midwifes the birth of Consciousness and Awareness and, in Her honour, ancient bards carried a golden branch of tinkling bells and they, along with the bards of today, sing praise poems to Her. 'Briathra Brighid' is the incantation by which the poet's mind is rendered prophetic:

> *Hail unto thee, Jewel of the Night!*
> *Beauty of the Heavens, Jewel of the Night!*
> *Mother of the Stars, Jewel of the Night!*
> *Foster Mother of the Sun, Jewel of the Night!*
> *Majesty of the Stars, Jewel of the Night!*

A LULLABY FOR BRIGHID'S CHILDREN

> *Inionaí, Inionaí*
> *Codailigi, Codailigi*
> *Inionaí, Inionaí*
> *Codailigi, Codailigi*

> *Codailigi, Codailigi*
> *Cois a chlé mo, Cois a chlé mo*

> *Codailigi, Codailigi*
> *Socair Sásta, Socair Sásta*

Little one, little one
Sleep, sleep
Little one, little one

Sleep, sleep.
Sleep, sleep
Upon my breast, upon my breast

Sleep, sleep
Peacefully serene, peacefully serene

As a daughter of the Tuatha de Danaan, Brighid is a fairy woman, perceived in sunbeams and moonbeams, starlight, candlelight, and hearthlight, Lady of the Healing Springs. She carries a white birch wand, the Tree of New Beginnings, bestowing renewal and grace wherever She walks.

Whenever it rains and her cloak gets wet, She hangs it on a sunbeam, causing a rainbow in the sky.

She is the Rainbow Bridge between cultures, ages, religions, and states of consciousness. She is adaptable and flexible, changing with the times so that she can always remain with the people.

Ways to give honour to Brighid and Her aspect of air:

- Wake up at dawn and greet the day; acknowledge Her presence in the rising Sun.
- Breathe Her in.
- Gather rushes and weave a Brighid's Cross.
- Lay a blue cloth out on Brighid's Eve, allowing it to be infused with Her healing mist. Keep it in a special place and use it for bathing fevers, bruises, rashes, burns, and abrasions.
- Write a poem; sing a song; listen to music; play music!
- Study something
- Teach what you learn. Be a mentor.
- Make an incense to nourish Her spirit in your space. Incense represents the breath of the divine and the carrying of your prayers out into the universe.

Elements of air

Time – dawn, new moon, spring.
Place – the east, mountain tops, the sky, the abyss, the void, space.
Powers and blessings – beginnings, breath, communication, sound, silence, hearing, listening, thinking, ideas, sight, vision, insight, imagination,

words, writing, reading, ogham, smell, weaving, singing, laughing, flying, clarity, inspiration, renewal, lightness.

Body systems – nervous system, respiratory system, endocrine system the brain, the mind, eyes, ears, throat.

Sound	Rune	Name	Tree	Attributes
B	⊢	Beth	Birch	Birth, beginnings, blessings
L	⊨	Luis	Rowan	Magic, renewal, recovery, regeneration
F	⊨	Fearn	Alder	Magical speech, keen intuition
S	⊨	Saille	Willow	The Moon Goddess, enchantment
N	⊨	Nuin	Ash	The World Tree – peace, wisdom, flexibility
H	⊣	Huath	Hawthorn	Love, sexuality, heart, positive change
D	⊣	Duir	Oak	The doorway – balance, strength, fortitude
T	⊣	Tinne	Holly	Personal sacrifice leading to growth and self-mastery
C	⊟	Coll	Hazel	Truth, visions of other realms
Q	⊟	Quert	Apple	The fruit of the Otherworld; love and regeneration
M	✛	Muin	Vine	Joy, awareness, abundance
G	✛	Gort	Ivy	Self-enlightenment and discovery
Ng	✚	Ngetal	Broom/reed	Overcoming fear of change
St	✚	Strait	Blackthorn	Breaks down and dissolves
R	✚	Ruis	Elder	Magic, mending, deepening
A	✛	Ailm	Fir	Objectivity, sovereignty
O	✚	Onn	Gorse/furze	New opportunities, positive change
U	✚	Ur	Heather/Mistletoe	Passion, fulfilment, home
E	✚	Eadha	Aspen	Strong intuition, group strength
I	✚	Idho	Yew	Birth, death, rebirth, spiritual understanding

Deities – Danu, Brighid, Aine, Rhiannon, Aongus Macog, Merlin, the Maiden and the Youth, the Divine Child.

Spirits – sylphs (wind spirits), fairies, angels, the wind.

Planets and signs – Gemini, Libra, Aquarius, Mercury.

Colours – white of clouds, blue of sky, lavender and pink of dawn, yellow of spring flowers.

Animals – birds, flying insects, bees, butterflies, spiders, dragonflies, the phoenix.

Plants – chamomile, lavender, rosemary, thyme, chickweed, skullcap, oatstraw, Coltsfoot, clary sage, wormwood, mugwort, broom, cedar, pine, vervain.

Stones – clear quartz, amythest, fluorite, celestialite.

Tools – astrology, the web, the blade, scissors, the sword, the silver branch, the broom, feathers, bow and arrow, lunar waters and flower essences, aromatherapy, incense.

Offerings – incense, seeds, feathers, scents, breath, song, poetry.

NURTURING THE SPIRIT OF AIR

The art of crafting incense

Incense represents the Divine Breath, carrying our prayers out into the Universe. Depending on the herbs used, they can bless or banish. Make blessing incenses during the waxing Moon (from New to Full) and banishing incenses in the waning Moon (Full to New). Work with the Lunar Astrology to determine more specific times (for example, you might want to make a Warrior incense during a Fire Moon, a household incense during an Earth Moon.) Using dried herbs, mix small batches at a time in a mortar and pestle (or in a bowl if you don't have one) and store in small glass jars in a dark place. Burn on incense charcoals (no, barbecue charcoal won't work!) in a fire-proof pot (a small metal cauldron with three legs and a handle works best). Include the Moon sign in which you made it on the label and keep notes in your journal as to how it affects your space and mood. Feel free to 'play' with the recipes – there is always a herb that can be substituted. Remember, it's the intent behind it that's most important.

Plants to honour and invoke Her

Dandelion leaves and flowers – an Caisearbhán

Strength, vitality, determination – to represent her guiding light.

Blackberry leaves and flowers – an Muir dubh

For nourishment, abundance and protection, growth and fertility.

Lady's mantle – Dearna Muire

The cloak of Bridé, for her blessings of protection and prosperity. Helps to create a sanctuary of the home.

Vervain – an Bheirbhéine

The holiest herb of the Tuatha and the Celts. Used at all ceremonies and festivals as incense, lustral water and altar offering to deepen the sense of the sacred and bring love, protection, health, wealth, and good fortune.

Mullein – Coinnle Muire

One of several plants that represent the light of Brighid. For enlightenment, awareness, insight, and consciousness. A guide through difficult or confusing times. The dried stalks can be soaked in fat or wax and used as torches.

Birch – Beth

(Leaves.) Birch is the tree out of which Brighid's white wand of renewal is crafted. Brings the blessings of new beginnings, regeneration, and rebirth.

Oak – Duir

The doorway between the realms. Bestows fertility and enduring beauty; balanced strength, courage, and the ability to stand firm, despite the odds. Cill Dara, the Gaelic form of Kildare, means Church of the Oak. The particular tree by which She built Her temple was considered so sacred that weapons were not allowed near it.

Wood betony

Dispels negativity, alleviates nightmares and anxious thoughts. Enhances consciousness and centredness. Alleviates paranoia and worry.

Nettles – an Neantog

Offers strength, protection, and respectability; one must approach nettles with respect and caution – if not, she will sting. If she is given the respect she deserves, the nourishment she offers is great. A role model for womanhood.

Yarrow – an Atheir Thalun

The following traditional chant, said while gathering yarrow, says it all:

> May I be an isle in the sea,
> May I be a hill on the shore,
> May I be a star in the waning of the moon,
> May I be a staff to the weak.
> Wound can I every man,
> Wound can no man me.

Brighid is attributed with the inventions of whistling, keening, and writing, so that we could communicate with people far away and they 'could hear us with their eyes'. This ancient system of writing is called the Ogham. See the table overleaf.

Celtia incense

I make quite a large batch of this mixture and use it as my basic incense for centring, grounding and honouring ancestors as it invokes the following blessings:

Mugwort – for the blessings of the Moon.
Borage – for the warrior's courage.
Mint – for prosperity and to clarify psychic abilities.
Mistletoe – for sacredness and rebirth.
Thyme – to invoke the Fairie.
Foxglove – for deep magic.
Vervain – to attract one's desires and to invoke the Divine; for love, health, wealth and protection, for the ancestors.

Purification and protection incense

1 part vervain – purifies and sanctifies – the protection of the ancestors
1 part oak leaves – the protection of dagda
1 part lady's mantle – the protection of Brighid
1 part wormwood – for peace and resolution
$\frac{1}{2}$ part sage – deep cleansing
$\frac{1}{2}$ part rosemary – respect and friendship

1 part thyme – powerfully cleansing, antiseptic and invites the fairie to come and dwell

Use when first moving into a house and as needed.

Health incense

1 part pine or fir needles
1 part thyme
1 part chamomile
1 part lavender

Burn in the sickroom and throughout the house in times of viral vulnerability. Cleansing and disinfecting, immune booster.

Household wealth incense

These are all plants of prosperity.

1 part peppermint
1 part coltsfoot
1 part fir tips
1 part bayberry
1 part comfrey
$\frac{1}{2}$ part sage
1 part vervain
$\frac{1}{2}$ part mandrake

Bansighe's blessing

Use when seeking a woman-fairie's guidance and blessing. Equal parts:

Thyme – for Fairie magic and to move through time
Apple blossoms – for the Lady of Avalon
Cowslip or primrose flowers – another favourite of the Fairie
Foxglove flowers to deepen magic
Wild pansies – to see magic

Sweet dream incense

$2\frac{1}{2}$ parts vervain
1 part lady's mantle – or 'Brighid's Cloak' – to protect from nightmares
1 part elder flowers – for bright dreams

$\frac{1}{2}$ part mugwort – for messages from the otherworld and the blessings of
the Moon

(do not use with children). Burn in your room $\frac{1}{2}$ hour before bedtime.
There will be other recipes as we go along.

THE NERVOUS SYSTEM

The psyche affects the body. The body affects the psyche.

Control and integration of the body's billions of cells are accomplished
mainly by two communication systems – the nervous system (via electrical nerve impulses) and the endocrine system (via chemical secretions
into the blood system). These impulses and secretions communicate
information to body structures, increasing or decreasing activities as
needed for healthy survival. Nerve cells transmit messages from one to
the other, processing external experience to regulate the inner being
(hence the importance of a harmonious environment!)

The nervous system is the internal, electrochemical, communications
network of the body. 47 miles of nerves carry 3 million messages per
second, literally making it the Internet of the body!

There are two main parts – the central nervous system (the CNS) and
the peripheral nervous system (the PNS).

The central nervous system is composed of the brain and spinal cord.

The brain

This is more complex than any computer. There are three main parts:

1. The brain stem or medulla, which controls vital functions or homeostasis – heartbeat, breathing, blood pressure.
2. The hindbrain or cerebellum, which controls muscles and balance,
   walking, running, etc.
3. The front brain or cerebrum, which the home of our personality, consciousness and memory – enables us to think, feel, learn, create.

If all other neurons were functioning normally and only the cerebral
neurons were not, then

(a) you could not think or use your will
(b) you could not remember anything that has ever happened to you
(c) you could not decide to make the smallest movement
(d) you could not see or hear

(e) nothing would anger or frighten you

(f) nothing would bring you joy or sorrow

(g) you could not experience sensations.

The spinal cord

This is the primary reflex centre of the body, carrying impulses to and from the brain, translating incoming sensory experiences to outgoing motor actions such as, for example, pulling one's hand away from a hot surface.

Sensory impulses travel *up* to the brain in ascending tracts. Motor impulses travel *down* in descending tracts. Therefore, if injury cuts the cord all the way across, impulses can no longer travel *to* the brain from any part of the body below the injury, nor can they travel *from* the brain to these parts, resulting in paralysis.

The peripheral nervous system is made up of all the nerves that run through the rest of the body. It is divided into the voluntary and involuntary systems:

1. The voluntary system facilitates chosen movements – walking, reaching, blinking, chewing, etc.
2. The involuntary system regulates, maintains and restores homeostasis, the vital functions of the body – breathing, heart rate, digestion and circulation.

The cells of the nervous system

There are two types:

1. Neurons, which conduct impulses.
2. Neuroglia (glia = glue), which are specialised connective tissue cells. They support the neurons, holding them together and protecting them.

Neurons have three parts:

1. The cell body.
2. Dendrites – branching projections that transmit impulses to the cell body.
3. Axons – tubule projections that transmit impulses away from the cell body.

There are three types of neuron:

1. Sensory neurons – transmit impulses to the spinal cord and brain from all parts of the body.

2. Motor neurons – transmit impulses away from the brain and spinal cord to muscle and glandular tissue.
3. Interneurons – conduct impulses from sensory to motor neurons.

HOW STRESS AFFECTS THE BODY

We all experience stress every day. The levels of stress that we can handle are relative to the individual. It is how we react to the stress that determines whether it will be detrimental. Chronic stress, ongoing without a break and no help or support eventually becomes acute stress. An acute stress can become chronic, such that the acute fear becomes chronic worry. Either way, the ultimate impact is a weakening of some part or parts of the body, leading to many kinds of 'dis-ease'.

During acute stress or a 'fight or flight' situation (where feelings of fear, anger, grief, anxiety are experienced):

- The heart rate and force of contraction increases.
- Blood is shunted away from the skin and internal organs, except the heart and lungs. Blood supply of oxygen and glucose to muscles and the brain is increased. (This is what allows us to 'fight or fly', but prolonged experience starves the skin and organs of blood.)
- Breath rate increases (causing stress on the heart and circulation, asthmatic symptoms).
- Sweat production increases (leading to dehydration).
- Digestive secretions are severely reduced (resulting in poor digestion and malabsorbtion of minerals).
- Blood sugar levels increase – the liver dumps glucose into the bloodstream.

Now, compare those stress responses to the body and psyche in a relaxed state:

- Heart rate and blood pressure are reduced.
- The heart beats more effectively.
- Blood is shunted towards internal organs, especially the digestive system.
- Rate of breathing reduces.
- Sweat production decreases.
- Digestion improves through increased digestive secretions.
- Blood sugar levels normalise.

Imbalances of the nervous system (brought on by sustained stress)

Angina

Anorexia nervosa (and other eating disorders)

Asthma

Autoimmune diseases

Cancer

Cardiovascular disease

Common cold

Depression

Diabetes (adult, type II)

Epilepsy

Eczema/skin disorders

Herpes

Hiccups

Hives

Hypertension

Insomnia

Irritability

Irritable bowel syndrome

Mental sluggishness/forgetfulness

Migraine and other headaches

Motion sickness

Multiple sclerosis

Muscle twitching/tics

Neuritis (peripheral neuropathy)

Parkinson's disease

PMS/menstrual discomfort

Rheumatoid arthritis

Sciatica

Tinnitus

Ulcerative colitis

So! As you can see, stress leads to many diseases. Therefore, addressing the nervous system and working to diminish and manage stress contributes a great deal towards healing and health, before we've even begun to address the specific disease or system affected!

Herbal support for stress

The plant world offers a wealth of allies to help smooth life's way. Prepared as teas, tinctures, incenses, oils, lotions and baths, it is as though the plant beings walk along with us, soothing and strengthening our weary bodies, minds and hearts.

Actions required to restore the body to a non-stress state

- Tonics – to strengthen and tone the nervous system: oatstraw, vervain, borage, sweet violet.
- Calming nervines or relaxants: lavender essential oil, chamomile, marjoram essential oil, vervain, motherwort, skullcap, wood betony.
- Nervine stimulants – for depression and fatigue (don't overuse!): rosemary, peppermint.
- Cardiac tonics – to nourish and strengthen the heart: hawthorn, borage, motherwort.

- Anti-spasmodics – for tight muscles and spasms: crampbark, skullcap, chamomile, sage.
- Anti-depressants (depression is often a secondary response to the initial stress event): lemon balm, lavender, clary sage, St. John's wort, rose.
- Adaptogens – help us to 'adapt' more gracefully to the situation. Good to use *before* the stress begins: nettles, borage, bitters.
- Analgesics – if pain is a symptom, e.g. tension headaches, muscle aches: crampbark, skullcap, lavender, willow bark.
- Hypnotics – to aid sleep: chamomile, marjoram, hops, passion flower, skullcap.

Possible formulas

Can be prepared as tea or tincture. Consider each 'part' as an ounce.

For general stress

Borage – 2 parts
Motherwort – 1 part
Oatstraw – 2 parts
Skullcap – 1 part [1 cup tea or 20 drops tincture 3 times per day]
Nettles – 2 parts

Supplies the following

Nervine tonic – all
Nervine relaxant – motherwort, skullcap
Bitter tonic – motherwort
Cardiac tonic – motherwort
Antispasmodic – skullcap

Acute stress with indigestion

Borage – 2 parts
Motherwort – 1 part
Oatstraw – 1 part
Chamomile – 2 parts
Meadowsweet – 2 parts

Acute stress with associated liver problems (e.g. alcoholism)

Add milk thistle or dandelion.

Acute stress with respiratory problems (e.g. asthma)

Add mullein, coltsfoot, fennel.

Acute stress with muscular problems

Add crampbark, damiana, wood betony.

Acute stress with skin inflammations

Add calendula.

Imbalances of the nervous system

Anxiety, characterised by

- An inability to relax.
- Emotional instability – a tendency to cry or be irritable with no obvious cause.
- Headache.
- Sleeplessness.

Actions indicated

- Nervine tonic.
- Nervine relaxant.
- Adrenal tonic (when anxious or panicking the adrenal glands secrete massive doses of adrenaline).
- Bitters – to aid the liver and digestive organs.
- Adaptogen.

Herbs – as tea or tincture

Skullcap, motherwort, vervain, chamomile, lemon balm.
Essential oils of sage, lemon balm, chamomile, lavender.

Possible formula

Oatstraw – 2 parts (nervine tonic)
Motherwort – 2 parts (nervine relaxant, bitter)
Borage – 2 parts (adrenal tonic) drink as needed up to
Dandelion – 2 parts (bitter, adaptogen) 6 cups a day
Essential oil inhalant of choice

Panic attacks, characterised by

- Heart palpitations.
- Intense feelings of fear.
- A feeling of impending doom.
- Breathlessness.

Herbs

Motherwort, wood betony, borage.
Administer as tincture – 20 drops or 1 tsp. every 20 minutes until symptoms subside.

DEPRESSION

A result of suppressed anger, grief or anxiety. Our shadow self is calling us down to the underworld, to go deep within ourselves, access those feelings and bring them up to the surface to be expressed and released. Herbs by themselves won't do it if we're not willing to do the internal work as well. The healing of depression requires a program of internal and external therapies.

Actions indicated

Nervine tonics
Nervine stimulant
Bitters
Adaptogen
System support (respiratory, digestive, etc., depending on the individual)

Possible formula

St. John's wort – 2 parts (stimulates secretion of seratonin and dopamine).
    Must be fresh – prepare as tincture.
Peppermint – 2 parts (nervine stimulant, soothes stomach).
Oatstraw – 1 part (nervine tonic).
Borage – 1 part (nervine tonic, adaptogen).
Dandelion – 2 parts (adaptogen, nutrient, digestive tonic – stimulate appetite). For food and for life!

ADDITIONAL THERAPIES

- Rescue remedy/flower essences.
- Aromatherapy – inhalants, baths, anointing oils: marjoram, lemon balm, sage, lavender, clary sage.
- Incense sage, vervain, lavender (equal parts).
- Soothing music, natural sounds (wind song, bird song flowing water).

- Warm baths.
- Meditation, prayer.
- Exercise – yoga, tai chi, etc.
- Massage.
- Easily digested foods – high in vitamins C and B.
- Laughter – the best medicine! Science has proven that laughter. Relaxes blood vessels, strengthens heart rate, lowers blood pressure, secretes endorphins and boosts immunity!
- Naps.
- Change of scenery.
- Familiar things.
- Forgiveness, tolerance, compassion, self-knowing.
- Perspective – is it really so serious? We have the power to choose how we react to any given situation, particularly the relatively minor daily stresses. We can train our minds and our egos to respond appropriately and save our energy for the bigger things in life. We can choose how and what we spend our energy on.

AROMATHERAPY

Aromatherapy for the environment

I am sure you have all used aromatherapy in your lives in some form or another? Maybe in a bath or lavender for a tension headache? We all know that these distilled essences of plants smell delicious and increase our emotional well being. However, that is only the beginning of the wonderful benefits of essential oils.

They can also be used very effectively for all the cleaning jobs in our homes instead of the toxic cocktail of chemical cleansers currently on the market, which are poisoning our waters and us too.

We absorb essential oils and synthetic chemicals through our skin and respiratory tract. When we use the chemical cleaners, we are absorbing:

- Nervous system depressants or stimulants.
- Narcotics.
- Carcinogens.
- Banned substances.
- Respiratory irritants.
- Hazardous wastes.
- Chloroform.

- Acetone.
- Ethanol.
- Formaldehyde and other irritants.

Continual exposure causes nervous system, respiratory, digestive and immune diseases.

The exciting evidence of 'Hertz frequency'

In 1992, Bruce Tainio, of Tainio Technology, a division of Eastern State University, determined that the electrical frequency of the healthy human body is 62–78 Hz (Hertz).

Every disease also has an electrical frequency. If the human body is running at the healthy frequency of 62–78 Hz, it can prevent and neutralise diseases of a lower frequency.

Stress, malnutrition and exposure to pollutants (this includes synthetic chemical household cleaners) will lower the frequency of the human body to 58 or below, compromising the immune system.

At 58 Hz, the body is vulnerable to colds and flu, which also measure at 58 Hz.

At 55 Hz, candida and other yeast infections can develop.

At 52 Hz, Epstein–Barr and other chronic viruses can enter the body.

At 42 Hz, cancer can develop.

Therefore, the lower the hertz frequency and vitality of the human body, the more serious the diseases it can fall prey to.

The good news is that plants also have an electrical frequency.

Processed/canned foods measure 0 Hz.
Fresh foods average around 15 Hz.
Dry herbs measure from 12 to 22 Hz.
Fresh herbs measure from 20 to 27 Hz.
Essential oils measure from 52 to 320 Hz.

So, eating fresh foods and herbs and employing the use of essential oils as aromatherapy all greatly boost the immune system and natural vitality.

But wait! There's more! All essential oils are anti-microbial and anti-inflammatory, the strength of these health-promoting actions depending on the particular plant. Their anti-microbial properties neutralise harmful bacteria without adding chemical pollutants to the environment.

Lemon, for example, has proven in laboratory tests to neutralise meningococcus in fifteen minutes and pneumococcus in one to three hours.

Thyme essential oil has proven to neutralise typhus and dysentery bacillus in two minutes, the tuberculosis bacillus in thirty to sixty minutes!

As a herbalist/aromatherapist for 21 years, I have seen more chronic fatigue, nervousness and headaches, hyperactivity in children, skin conditions and respiratory diseases clear up simply with the elimination of chemical household cleaners. As my clients switched to natural, eco-friendly products, they became healthier, physically and emotionally. Additional benefits included knowing they were doing something good for the environment and everyone else in the household, including pets, were healthier and happier!

My favourite method of employment is a spray bottle, which I fill with water and add my selection of essential oils, about 20 drops to 1 pint of water. I use this to clean kitchen and bathroom surfaces and floors, mirrors, glass, tiles, even my car! Of course, it also deodorises at the same time!

Essential oils are highly concentrated plant essences, requiring large amounts of organic material to obtain a small amount of pure oil. When purchasing, look for '100% pure essential oil'. Beware of marketing ploys such as 'escentual oil'. These are not derived from natural sources, and are often synthesised perfumes. In addition, try to buy only products that list the botanical name as well as the common name on the label, to ensure accuracy.

All essential oils are anti-inflammatory and anti-microbial to a degree and work through the sense of smell and the absorption of the skin, affecting the brain and nervous system, which ultimately affects the rest of the body's organs. Their scents evoke memories, visions, energies, and therefore skilful blending is important to promote a positive experience. Essential oils are *very* concentrated and *very* potent, so work with a light hand. Do not ingest essential oils without very specific training.

Except for lavender and tea tree, essential oils should always be placed in a carrier liquid of some kind.

For general use: 2% dilution (10 drops per ounce of carrier). For babies and sensitive skin: 1% dilution (5–6 drops per ounce).

Carrier oils

Almond (my favourite for anointing and massage oils), sesame, olive (my favourite for medicinal oils), avocado, safflower, sunflower.

Methods of application

Massage oil – 2% dilution.
Bath 2–10 drops per bath depending on skin sensitivity.
Douche, enema, footbath – 5–10 drops per quart.

Compress or mouthwash – 2 drops per $\frac{1}{2}$ cup of water.

Steam inhalant – 5 drops per quart of water. Alternatively, sprinkle 1-2 drops on a hankie, pillowcase or cottonball.

Spray bottle – 10–20 drops per pint of water. I make one to use as a natural air-freshener and cleaning agent using 8 drops of lavender, 6 drops of lemon, 6 drops of thyme.

Essential oils

Anise (*Pimpinella anisum*): Herb of Air
Relaxing expectorant, antispasmodic. Anise heals the lungs. Use the herb in steams and tea with honey for coughs. Drinking the tea or anointing with the essential oil before divination exercises strengthens psychic abilities.

Chamomile (*Anthemis nobilis, Matricaria* spp.): Herb of Air/Gentle Fire
Strong anti-inflammatory and anti-spasmodic. Relaxing, calming, soothing to the nerves, stimulates physical and psychic digestion, relieves pain and aids sleep. Empowers the solar plexus and soothes the inner child. Excellent in babycare recipes.

Clary sage (*Salvia sclerea*): Herb of Air
Uplifting and relaxing, anti-depressant. Quiets negative thoughts and elevates mood, even to euphoria. One drop rubbed into the temples is an excellent remedy for pre-menstrual tension. (Only one drop – more could cause headache!)

Eucalyptus (*Eucalyptus globulus*): Herb of Air
Respiratory anti-inflammatory, circulatory stimulant. Healing for coughs, asthma, bronchitis, catarrhal discharge and fever. Use in steams and salves.

Lavender (*Lavendula off./Augustifolia*): Herb of Air
Cleansing, antiseptic, anti-inflammatory. Excellent for skin problems, incredibly healing for burns (assuming it is the true *Lavendula officianalis* or *Augustifolia*). Tension reducer, pain reliever, physical and mental anti-depressant. Sleep enhancer. Lavender 'clears the air'. It is one of my favourites to use in my spray bottle.

Marjoram (*Oreganum marjorama*): Herb of Water, the Heart
Deeply sedative, anti-spasmodic, soothing. Lowers neural receptivity, increases sensual threshold, even in sexual matters. Soothing to an anxious heart.

Rose geranium (*Pelargonium capitatum*): Herb of Water/Earth
Anti-inflammatory for skin, dermatitis, haemorrhoids. Neutralises, balances, harmonises the heart and physical body. Add to creams and

lotions for mature skin. Increases sense of happiness, awareness of love and beauty. Can substitute for rose oil.

Rosemary (*Rosemarinus off.*): Herb of Air
Stimulating and energizing, provides mental clarity and strengthens memory. An excellent ally for students, helping us to remember what we learn! Strengthening in cases of weakness, lack of motivation, rosemary provides a second wind at the end of a long day. Enhances the will and determination. Promotes communication and friendship.

Sage (*Salvia off.*): Herb of Earth
Grounding, centring, balancing. Strengthens stamina. Strengthens the voice. Anti-inflammatory for teeth and gums. Anti-itch.

Spikenard (*Aralia racemosa, Californica*): Herb of Earth
Provides strength and grounding, excellent for overwhelm. Aids birth and delivery.

RESPIRATION

Breath is life. Breath is spirit

Inspiration – to be filled with spirit; a sudden creative idea or act, guided by divine influence. Exultation – to be filled with joy, to raise to a higher consciousness.

Functions of the respiratory system

The distribution of air/oxygen = inspiration.
A gas exchanger – removes carbon dioxide = expiration.
Filters, warms and humidifies the air.
A haemostatic mechanism.
Influences speech.
Makes smell possible.

The journey down your windpipe

Upper respiratory

Nose – hair and mucus trap dust/dirt particles.
Warms and moisturises the air.
Contains sense organs of smell.
Nasal cavities (sinuses) – lined with epithelium cells which secrete mucus.
Lymph tissue.
Adds timbre to the voice.

Pharynx – passageway for food, liquids, air.

Larynx – the voice box – vocal cords are 'played' by expiration.

Epiglottis – flap of tissue that prevents food passage – opens to allow air through.

Trachea – the windpipe.

Lower respiratory

The basic plan of the respiratory system would be that of an upside down tree, with the upper representing the trunk, the lower representing the branches and leaves.

The lungs

Bronchi – the main branches. Two main tubes, one for each lung, made of smooth muscle and mucus membrane.

Bronchioles – the branches of the tree.

Alveoli – the fruit of the tree. Where carbon dioxide is exchanged for oxygen. The 'gas station' – red blood cells (the trucks) arrive empty of oxygen and load up with more. There are 7 million alveoli, each the size of a pinhead. They have delicate thin walls which allow oxygen and carbon dioxide to pass through – the exchange of gases. If they were spread out, they would cover a tennis court.

Ribcage – surrounds and protects.

Pleura – the protective covering of the lungs. Alleviates friction while breathing. Upon inspiration, the rib muscles shorten, pulling ribs upward and outward. The diaphragm shortens, pulling down, making the chest/lung cavity bigger, allowing air to fill the space created. Upon expiration, the rib muscles relax and lengthen, allowing the diaphragm to move up, pushing air out. Good posture is very important for good breathing.

Mucous membrane – lines the entire respiratory tract. Serves as an air purifier, moisturiser, is anti-inflammatory and anti-microbial.

THE RESPIRATORY SYSTEM – ACTIONS AND *MATERIA MEDICA*

Tonics – to strengthen the function and tissues.
Coltsfoot, mullein, horehound, hyssop, comfrey.

Anti-microbials – to banish bacterial infections.
Thyme, lemon balm, sage, eucalyptus, garlic, onion, raw honey, yarrow, elecampane, anise, fennel.

Anti-virals – to alleviate viral infections present in colds, flu, bronchitis. Notice that many herbs are anti-microbial and anti-viral, allowing us to treat the illness without having to determine which it is – let's see, is this a virus or a bacterial infection? Thyme, lemon balm, horehound, St. John's wort, garlic.

Astringents – strengthen the integrity of respiratory tissue.
Sage, nettles, prunella, elecampane, yarrow, lungwort.

Anti-catarrhals – alleviate excess mucus.
Sage, nettles, mullein, coltsfoot, mallow, elecampane, fennel.

Anti-inflammatories
Thyme, sage, nettles, marjoram, prunella, honey, mullein, coltsfoot, mallow, cowslip, fennel.

Anti-spasmodics
Thyme, marjoram, cowslip, coltsfoot, horehound, hyssop, lemon balm, honey, fennel.

Diaphoretics/febrifuge
Yarrow, ginger, cayenne, catnip, boneset, elder flowers, hyssop, elecampane, lavender.

Demulcents
Mullein, coltsfoot, mallow, comfrey, cinnamon, honey.

Relaxing expectorants
Mullein, coltsfoot, comfrey, mallow, cowslip, horehound, hyssop, fennel.

Stimulating expectorants
Horehound, elecampane, fennel, bloodroot.

Cardio-tonics
Hawthorn, motherwort, marjoram.

Lymphatics
Cleavers, calendula, red clover, apple cider vinegar.

Digestive tonics
Thyme, horehound, basil, marjoram, rosemary.

Anti-asthmatics
Fresh nettles, apple cider vinegar and honey.

RESPIRATORY THERAPIES

Tonic tea

Fennel – 1 part
Mullein – 1 part
Coltsfoot – 1 part
Hawthorn – 1 part
Rose hips – 1 part
1 cup three times a day.

Fennel/aniseed syrup

Combine 1 cup of fennel or anise seed with 1 quart of water in a saucepan. Bring to a boil and simmer gently for 30 minutes.

Strain and cool. Stir in $\frac{1}{2}$ cup honey. Bottle, label and store in refrigerator. Take by the tablespoonful as needed for cough.

Head cold

Thyme – 1 part
Rosemary – 1 part
Sage – $\frac{1}{2}$ part
Infuse for 30 minutes. Add 1 tsp. Honey per cup. 3–4 cups a day for an adult. Continue for two days after symptoms subside.
Add onions, garlic and/or horseradish to food.

Sore throat

Gargle with

1 drop sage essential oil
1 tsp. sea salt

in 4 oz. water every 4 hours.

Colds, flu, bronchitis with fever

Tea
Thyme – 1 part
Elder flowers – 1 part
Yarrow – 1 part
30 minute infusion. Do *not* add sweetener. 1 cup every four hours for an adult.

Half dosage for a child of 75 lbs (5 stone).

Sponge bath

Make tea as above and add 3 drops lavender essential oil per cup. Bathe every four hours during high temperature.

Chest rub

1 drop thyme essential oil
2 drops sage essential oil
2 drops marjoram essential oil
Mixed into 1 oz. carrier oil

Earache

6 drops lavender essential oil in 1 oz. carrier oil
Apply 1 or 2 drops in each ear every 8 hours. Plug with cotton. Or garlic oil capsule – puncture with pin. Apply as above.

Asthma

Fresh nettle tea – 1 cup with raw local honey every 4 hours. More often if needed. Or fresh nettle tincture – 1 tsp. mixed with 1 cup water and 1–2 tsps. honey every 4 hours. More often if needed. Also use chest rub.

WEAVING THE WEB

Suggestions for working with the element of Air and the lessons of this chapter

Make an altar to honour and empower the spirit of Air. Greet Brighid each morning and observe any shifts in your self and your day. Record your reactions.

Harvest and dry (if you can) and/or buy the plants you'd like to have in an incense.

Make an incense appropriate to your needs. Work with appropriate Moon phases. Burn it daily for a week and observe the responding energies. Make an incense of Air to empower vision, communication, and insight. Make an offering to the Winds of the Four Directions (an incense is traditional but feel free to be unique and creative – both please the Lady).

Make a personal aromatherapy blend. Anoint yourself with it at the beginning of your day, refreshing as often as you wish to, and observe your responding energies, emotions, etc.

Give yourself some time to spend in contemplation and meditation, two very nurturing and empowering activities.

Contemplate your own stress levels and create a nervous system programme for yourself using herbs and additional therapies. Remember, we try everything on ourselves before suggesting it to others! Include a herbal tea and/or tincture and therapies that address the mental, emotional, physical and spiritual aspects.

Try out some of the respiratory recipes on yourself, friends and family as the season's colds and flus come on. Keep careful notes on what is taken and the resulting reactions.

Contemplate the Ogham. Try to sit for a while with any of the trees that call to you. Take the Spirit of the Tree a gift. Write your name in Ogham. Make one long vertical line. Then make the letters by making the cross marks, beginning at the bottom and working up. Contemplate the trees that make up your name. These are your power trees. The Ogham can be embroidered, carved, painted, etc. Into your sacred objects to further empower and focus them.

Obtain some nettles, borage and thyme and work with each of them for a week at a time in different ways. Acquaint yourself with the three herbs as tea, incense, and any other way you are inspired to. Record your experiences.

CHAPTER 3

LADY OF FIRE

As the Sacred Flame that gives us light and warmth, Brighid dwells in candlelight, hearthlight, and the Sun that rises every day. She guards and teaches the blacksmiths, as they work with the sacred fire to transform metal into useful tools. The smiths are greatly honoured in Celtic culture and the water of their forges is used to cure warts and other blemishes. When we, as a people, are ready to lay down our weapons of destruction, Brighid and her smiths will help us forge them into tools of peace.

Nineteen priestesses guarded Her sacred shrine in Kildare; nineteen, the number of years it takes for the New Moon to coincide with the Winter Solstice, emphasising both her lunar and solar nature. This flame, wherein dwells Brighid, is a guide through the darkness and reflects the divine spark within each of us. The flame also reflects the warmth and brightness of Her personality as well as Her unconditional love and desire to give aid.

A chant for greeting Her on the rising sun

> Brighid, excellent woman,
> Sudden flame
> May the bright fiery Sun
> Take us to the Lasting Kingdom

FROM THE BOOK OF LISMORE

On a certain day the bondmaid went to milk her kine, and left the girl (Brighid) sleeping in her house. Certain neighbours beheld the house, wherein the girl lay, ablaze, so that one flame was made thereof from earth to heaven. When they came to rescue the house, there was no fire, but they saw that the girl was full of the grace of the Holy Spirit.

One day the wizard was sitting with Brighid in a certain place, and the cow-dung which lay before the girl they beheld ablaze. When they stretched their hands out to it, there was no fire.

In Her fire aspect, Brighid carries a sword, the Blade of Truth and Justice. She abhors war and offers Her protection to soldiers who will lay down their weapons. She is a mediator of princes and Kings, helping to preserve peace upon the land. She is the protector of the weak and vulnerable. She dispenses the Laws that ensure the good of all.

During Her incarnation as St. Brigid, She dedicated Herself as a free woman to the religious life. She stalwartly stood by Her principles, even though She had many suitors for her hand in marriage as illustrated by this story:

> *A particularly persistent man came to ask Brighid's father
> and her brothers to give Her to him in marriage. They
> approached Brighid with this proposal and once again She
> refused, for She wanted to found a healing centre to take care
> of the poor and sick. One brother said, 'What good is that
> pure eye in your head if it's not looking across the pillow at a
> husband?'*
>
> *This angered and humiliated Brighid and, sticking Her
> finger in Her eye, She pulled it out of its socket and let it lay
> hanging on Her cheek by a few sinews. Upon seeing what
> She was willing to do to fulfil Her convictions, Her father
> and brothers promised that never again would they press Her
> to marry and they would respect and support Her decision.*

In Her aspect of Fire, Brighid is our protector and the Lady of Justice. If we ask Her, she will protect us from those who would harm us. The following is an adaptation of a traditional Invocation for Justice that can be recited when one feels in danger. Stand with the Sun shining on you and say:

Brighid, I am bathing my face.
In the nine rays of the Sun,
As Mary bathed the Son
In generous milk fermented.

Sweetness be in my face,
Riches be in my countenance,
Comb-honey be on my tongue,
My breath as the incense.

Evil is yonder house,
Evil are those therein,
I am the White Swan,
Queen over them.

I will go in the name of Brighid,
In likeness of deer, in likeness of horse,
In likeness of serpent, in likeness of King,
More victorious am I than all persons.

It is a grave responsibility to deem someone evil. Many have been called so unjustly. But if the danger is true, Brighid will bring swift justice and protect you from harm. At other times the first, second, and fourth verses may be recited to empower your self-esteem.

A long time ago, before the invention of gas and electric power, fire was considered to be sacred. It gave us warmth, cooked our food, and illuminated our way through the darkness. It was considered by our ancient forebears to be a gift from the gods. The following invocation can be chanted over the kindling or a candle-flame, a hearthfire or a communal bonfire to acknowledge and evoke the sacred powers of the Spirit of Fire:

Go geosnai tirte fhaire Bhride
Muid ag na-hoibre
(Let the watchflames of Brighid
Guard us in our work)

Go ndo tinnáil rabhaidh Bhride
Muid a ghiollacht tri na scaileanna
(Let the signal fires of Brighid
burn to guide us through the shadows)

Go lasa laistigh bruane coranach Bhride
Agus ceangail muid le ne dheithe.
(Let the crowning flames of Brighid
Spark within and link us to the Gods.)

BRIGHID'S FIRE

An anointing oil to evoke Her protection and Her blessings

Take equal portions of dried yarrow, rosemary, lemon balm, borage, and vervain flowers and fill a jar halfway. Cover with borage seed or sunflower oil to the top of the jar. Cap and place in a sunny window for the three days and nights of the Full Moon. Strain through muslin cloth and pour into a beautiful bottle. Use to anoint your person, doorways to homes and businesses, amulets, and candles.

Ways to honour Brighid and Her aspect of Fire

- Light a candle – invite Brighid into your home.
- Kindle a hearthfire – offer herbs to its Spirit.
- Get up at dawn and greet the rising Sun.
- Kindle a community bonfire to bless the Season, the planting, the harvest.
- Do something that requires courage.
- Stand in protection of somebody weaker than you.
- Take a stand for a good cause.
- Pray for peace, protest war.
- Change for the better.

ELEMENTS OF FIRE

Time – Noon, waxing moon, summer.

Place – The south, deserts, volcanoes.

Powers and blessings – Light, warmth, creativity, passion, desire, dancing, courage, determination, changing, digestion, self-esteem, confidence, vitality, protection, purification, cleansing, clearing, enlightening, illuminating, truth, justice, sovereignty.

Body systems – digestive system, immune system.

Deities – Brighid, Grainne, the Sun Goddess, Lugh, the Sun King, Maeve, Queen of Connaught, Bel, God of Fire, Macha, Finn McCool, Warriors and Amazons.

Spirits – Salamanders, dragons, the phoenix, the sun.

Planets and signs – Aries, Leo, Sagittarius, Mars, the Sun.

Colours – Yellow of mustard flowers, gold of the sun, orange of sunsets, red of molten lava, blue flame of protection, white hot.

Animals – Predators, lions, cats, hawks, eagles, lizards, dragons, horses.

Plants – Borage, horsetail, St. John's wort, nettles, calendula, daisy, dock, dandelion, rue, blackberry, chamomile, lemon balm, yarrow, horseradish, elecampane, mullein, sunflowers, thistles, thyme, garlic, onions.

Stones – Citrine, carnelian, topaz, red jasper, garnet, fire opal, amber.

Tools – The wand, the censor, candles, oils, the torch, the spear, the hearth.

Offerings – Anointing oils, candles, burning anything.

THE DIGESTIVE SYSTEM

From mouth to anus, the digestive system is a hollow tube, measuring about 30 feet in an adult. It includes the gastro-intestinal tract (the GI tract), the salivary glands, liver, gall bladder and pancreas.

The walls of the tract are made of four different layers:

1. The mucosa – mucous membranes – contains anti-bacterial substances and protects against inflammation. The integrity of this mucosal lining is very important for digestive health. Demulcent herbs feed and strengthen the mucous membranes.
2. The sub-mucosa – connective tissue containing blood, lymph and nerve vessels.
3. The muscularis – layers of muscles in the intestinal walls.
4. The serosa – the outermost covering.

Digestion is physical (crushing and grinding), mixing food with chemicals (digestive juices, including enzymes).

Parts of the digestive system

The mouth – consists of the hard palette in the front and the soft palette at the back.

The 'uvula' – the 'hangy-down' thing in the back of the throat – keeps food and liquid from going up the nasal cavity.

The teeth – chew and masticate the food into a 'bolus'.

Saliva – contains the enzyme amylase and breaks down starch molecules.

Saliva is produced by the sublingual, submandibular and parotid salivary glands.

Upon swallowing, the bolus passes the uvula to the pharynx, then to the oesophagus – a 10-inch long muscular tube – which pushes the food down to the stomach.

The stomach – secretes gastric acid (hydrochloric acid) and various hormones and enzymes, and breaks down proteins and ionises minerals.

The stomach has two sphincters (muscular 'rings' that open and close to allow passage of food): the cardiac sphincter between the oesophagus and the stomach and the pyloric sphincter between the stomach and small intestine.

When empty, the stomach is the size of a large sausage. It consists of three types of muscle – circular, longitudinal and oblique (diagonal). These muscles churn food while adding hydrochloric acid and pepsin. Secretions are affected by hormones and vagus nerve impulses. Anger increases secretions. Fear and depression decrease secretions.

More health problems arise from the lack of gastric secretions.

The stomach can store up to 1 quart of food for an average of 3 hours.

The bolus then becomes semifluid chyme and is released into the small intestine, which secretes a variety of digestive and protective substances and receives the secretions of the liver, gall bladder and pancreas.

The small intestine is 20 feet long! Divided into three segments, the folds, villi and microvilli increase the absorbing surface 600 times! Villi and microvilli are tiny little 'fingers' that absorb nutrients into the bloodstream.

The duodenum – the first 4–12 inches – is a major site of chemical digestion and absorption of minerals. Mucus is produced for lubrication and protection. A hormone called secretin is released and sent to the pancreas, telling it to secrete alkaline juices to buffer acids.

The jejunum – 8 feet long – absorbs water-soluble vitamins, carbohydrates and proteins.

The ileum – 12 feet long – absorbs fat-soluble vitamins, fat, cholesterol and bile salts.

Malabsorption in the small intestine leads to nutrient deficiency. Celiac, food allergies and Chron's are diseases of malabsorption.

Segmentation of the small intestine brings the chyme into contact with the intestinal wall eliciting a nervous or parasympathetic response called peristalsis. Food then spirals through the intestine. It will pass to the ileococcal valve, which is the gateway to the large intestine, or colon – 5 feet in length – which is divided into four segments. They are the ascending colon, the transverse colon, the descending colon, and the sigmoid colon.

In the colon, final absorption of water, electrolytes and limited amounts of digestive proteins takes place. Vitamins K and B complex are manufactured here. Chyme is broken down into faeces within 3–10 hours. The colon converts any remaining proteins into amino acids.

The sigmoid colon is where faeces are held and lubrication is added. This mixture is sent to the rectum and anal canal for elimination.

The pancreas lies just behind the stomach, regulating blood sugar and releasing enzymes into the small intestine. Pancreatic juices consist of water, salts, sodium bicarbonate and enzymes with a pH of 7.1 to 8.2.

Their release is triggered by nerve and hormonal responses and they alkalise the stomach acids. $2\frac{1}{2}$ pints are secreted daily.

The enzymes include lipase, which digests fat and fat-soluble vitamins; protease, which digests proteins into amino acids and keeps the small intestine free of parasites (bacteria, yeast, protozoa, worms); amylase, which digests starch into smaller sugars; and sucrase, maltase and lactase, which break down vegetable and milk sugars into glucose, fructose and galactose.

Within the pancreas are the Islets of Langerhans, which secrete the hormones glucagon and insulin, responsible for blood sugar balance.

The gall bladder stores and concentrates the bile that is secreted by the liver into the duodenum.

HERBS AND ACTIONS FOR THE DIGESTIVE SYSTEM

Tonics: for overall health and strengthening. Bitters! Bitters! Bitters! and/ or whole dandelion, chamomile, fennel, daisy, marshmallow, thyme, comfrey, elecampane.

Demulcents: to nourish the mucosal lining of the entire gastro-intestinal tract. Mallow, marshmallow, comfrey, borage, oats, cinnamon.

Bitters: encourage secretions of all the digestive juices. Dandelion, dock, chamomile, agrimony, yarrow etc.

Astringents: strengthen and tone the gastro-intestinal muscles. Yarrow, agrimony, meadowsweet, rosehips, blackberry, nettles, wild geranium, strawberry leaf, lady's mantle, borage.

Antacids: Fennel, meadowsweet.

Relaxants: to ease tightness, cramps and spasms.

Carminatives: to alleviate bloating and gas. Chamomile, dill, peppermint, anise, fennel, marjoram, rosemary, thyme, sage, basil.

Laxatives: to correct constipation. Dandelion root, dock root, burdock root, psyllium seeds. (Demulcents help also in dry conditions.)

Hepatics/chologogues: Dandelion root, dock root, milk thistle, bitters.

Nervines: for stress-related digestive problems. Chamomile, borage, oats, marjoram, hops.

Anti-microbials: to deal with digestive tract infections, e.g. food poisoning. Thyme, horehound, garlic, chamomile, lemon balm, yarrow.

Anti-virals: to clear viruses, e.g. stomach flu. Thyme, horehound, lemon, balm, yarrow, garlic, St. John's wort.

Anthelmintic/vermifuge: to eliminate intestinal worms. Thyme, garlic, wormwood.

Emetics: cause vomiting, used to purge non-caustic poisons from the stomach. Lobelia, vervain (in high doses).

Anti-emetics: alleviate nausea. Chamomile, feverfew, peppermint, thyme.

Vulneraries: to heal gastro-intestinal wounds and ulcers. Calendula, yarrow.

DIGESTIVE SYSTEM THERAPIES

Indigestion

Indigestion is caused by irregular eating, eating too much, too rapidly, eating when anxious, angry, etc. or eating the wrong food.

The symptoms are bloating, 'heaviness', gas, dull pain and heartburn. These can be relieved by bitter teas before a meal, which will stimulate appetite and digestive activity.

Correct the cause – eat regularly, eat smaller meals more often, slow down, eliminate 'trigger' foods, fast (moderately) when experiencing anger or anxiety.

Soothe the digestive tract with infusions of one of the following: Fennel, chamomile, meadowsweet, mallow, marshmallow.

Diarrhoea

Diarrhoea is usually caused by infection or irritation of part of the digestive tract, sometimes accompanied by nausea and vomiting. This is the body's way of expelling the infection-causing bacteria. Like fever, it needs to be managed, rather than eliminated.

If we use too much astringency to 'dry it up', we will cause the bacteria to remain harboured in the gastro-intestinal tract and the illness to last longer.

Attention needs to be on replacing lost fluids and electrolytes, anti-microbial action for any infection, demulcents to support the mucous membranes and astringents to support the muscular walls.

To replace lost nutrients, use nettle tea with honey, cooked apple sauce with cinnamon, and water!

Use thyme, yarrow, lemon balm, horehound, or rosemary as anti-microbials.

As astringents, use nettles, yarrow, blackberry, agrimony, or wild geranium to strengthen muscular walls and slow down diarrhoea

Mallow, marshmallow, comfrey, borage, fennel and honey can be used as demulcents to soothe mucous membranes.

A possible recipe

Nettles – 2 parts – provides nutrients, astringent.
Thyme – 1 part – anti-microbial.
Mallow – 1 part – demulcent.
3 cups of tea a day. Supplement with additional teas, soups and lots of
water.

Constipation

Constipation results from poor diet, particularly lack of bitters and fibre, lack of water, lack of exercise, poor muscular action and/or nervous tension.

Add more bitters, vegetables for fibre and water to the diet.

Use 1 tsp. psyllium seeds in $\frac{1}{4}$ cup fruit juice, followed with 2 glasses of water to cleanse and lubricate the intestinal tract and stimulate elimination.

Basic laxative tea: Equal parts dock root and dandelion root tea (1 cup) or tincture (1 tsp. with water) before bed. For muscular weakness, incorporate tonic, astringent and demulcent actions. For example: nettle leaf as a tonic and astringent, with borage as a demulcent, in equal parts, 3 cups a day.

For nervous tension, incorporate relaxant, calming nervine and demulcent action. For example, 2 parts each of chamomile as a relaxant, bitter, calming nervine; borage as a nervine and demulcent, and mallow as a demulcent. Drink 3 cups a day.

LOW GASTRIC ACIDITY

This is the most common cause of digestive problems – the stomach doesn't produce enough acid to properly break down food.

Common symptoms

Bloating, belching, burning, flatulence
Extreme sense of fullness after eating moderately
Indigestion, diarrhoea, constipation
Food allergies
Nausea after taking supplements
Rectal itching

Chronic signs of low gastric acidity:

Weak, peeling, cracked fingernails
Dilated blood vessels in cheeks and nose
Acne
Iron deficiency
Chronic intestinal parasites
Undigested food in stool
Chronic candida
Upper digestive tract problems

Diseases associated with low gastric acidity:

Asthma
Celiac
Acne
Herpes
Eczema
Gallbladder disease
Chronic auto-immune disorders
Hepatitis
Hives
Lupus
Osteoporosis
Anaemia
Psoriasis
Rheumatoid arthritis
Rosaceae
Hyperthyroidism and hypothyroidism

Lack of bitter in the diet is the most common cause. Drink a bitter tea before meals, three times a day. Introduce more deep, leafy greens (mildly bitter) into the diet.

Gastritis

Inflammation of the stomach lining, resulting from the same causes as indigestion

Symptoms: Heartburn, vomiting, abdominal pain.

Therapies: Change diet – avoid caffeine, alcohol, sugars, fried foods and refined flour. Reduce stress, eat regularly, eat smaller meals more often.

Do not use Tums or other pharmaceutical antacids – these lay a chalky lining on the intestinal wall, diminishing the villi and preventing absorption of nutrients.

Actions to consider

Demulcent
Antacid
Anti-inflammatory
Astringent
Vulnerary
Nervine
Alterative (if chronic)

DOCTRINE OF SIGNATURES – FORM

Remember that these things can tell *what* they affect, not *how*!

Large leaves reflect lungs and skin, e.g. comfrey and elecampane.

Hairy leaves reflect the villi or cillia in the lungs and intestines, e.g. comfrey, marshmallow, and borage.

Thick leaves are often high in mucilage, e.g. marshmallow, mallow, and plantain.

Resinous leaves hold things together, like cut skin, loosen mucus and bring it to the surface.

Heart-shaped leaves obviously reflect the heart and may help to heal emotional and physical dis-eases.

Leaf veinings: Beginning with one large tube breaking into two, which break into two and so on, reflect the bronchioles. One long tube running the length of the leaf, with many smaller ones branching off, reflect the nervous system, e.g. borage and clary sage. Finely toothed leaves also can reflect the nervous system, e.g. lavender (calming) and rosemary (stimulating).

White sap can diminish consciousness, e.g. wild lettuce, and/or can indicate the presence of lactic acid which, when applied to warts, makes them disappear, e.g. dandelion.

White roots and flowers can help to heal bones, e.g. comfrey (root) and boneset (flowers).

Umbel flowers are often good for the lungs, reflecting the alveoli, e.g. yarrow and fennel.

Tubular stalks reflect bronchials, blood vessels, intestines, e.g. elder and marshmallow.

CRAFTING MEDICINAL OILS

Infused oils

To make an infused oil, first choose your carrier, known as 'fixed oils'. Possible choices are listed below.

Olive: My favourite for medicinal purposes. It is good for all skin types, including babies and the elderly. Its nourishing properties are easily absorbed through the skin. It is demulcent, emollient, anti-inflammatory and lubricant, healing for abrasions, bites, burns, muscle and joint pain. Obtained from the fruit, olive oil contains about 75% oleic acid, a monounsaturated fatty acid.

Almond oil: Excellent for mature and sensitive skin. Nourishing and revitalising, almond oil relieves dryness, itchiness, inflammation and soreness. Obtained from the kernel, it is lightweight and odourless and my choice for cosmetic and anointing oils to which essential oils are added.

Hazelnut oil: Rich in vitamins, mineral and proteins, lightweight and non-greasy, hazelnut is good for all skin types, especially dry or damaged, and is stimulating to circulation.

Apricot kernel oil: High in vitamins (especially A) and minerals, this oil is great for sensitive, inflamed, dry and prematurely aged skin. Lightweight, with a nice texture, it is suitable for body oils and lotions.

Plan to make your oils when the Moon is in a fire or an air sign. This helps to ensure that your oils will not go mouldy.

Making a fresh plant oil

Gather the plant on a dry, sunny day. Allow wilting for a few hours. This removes the water in the plant, which can contribute to moulding. Fill a jar with your plant material, which you have broken down into small pieces.

Flowers may be kept whole. Next, cover with your carrier oil to the top of the jar. Using a chopstick or the end of a wooden spoon, poke it down into the jar a few times to remove air bubbles. Cap and put in a warm, sunny window for a minimum of 3 days, maximum 2 weeks. Sunlight 'cooks' the oil. Strain and pour into a clean bottle and store in a cool place.

Making a dry plant oil

Fill a jar to one-third with your chosen plant. Next fill the jar to the top with your carrier oil. Remove air bubbles. Cap and put in a warm, sunny window for a minimum of one week, maximum 2 weeks. Strain; pour into a clean bottle and store in a cool place.

Herbs to consider

Calendula: The flowers are anti-inflammatory, anti-fungal, vulnerary, cosmetic. Excellent in a salve for diaper-rash.

Comfrey: The leaf-infused oil is the most quickly healing for abrasions and bruises sore muscles and bones. DO NOT use on deep cuts, as it will heal the surface skin so quickly that the deeper part of the wound will fester. Ideal for ageing skin in cosmetic preparations to alleviate fine lines and wrinkles. Comfrey is a cell proliferator, helping old cells to slough off and new ones to grow. Use dry plant as it can go mouldy easily.

Plantain: Gather the leaves and infuse for an anti-inflammatory oil that draws out impurities.

St. John's wort: Use leaves and flowers (must be fresh) to make an oil that heals burns and deep bruises. It should turn red during the infusion process.

Herbal salves

Once you have made your infused oils, you will then have the main ingredient for making your salves. The basic recipe is always one cup of infused oil and $\frac{1}{4}$ cup of grated beeswax, gently melted together over low heat and poured into jars. (Keep your beeswax in the freezer for easier grating.) Then, you can start mixing and matching with your various oils and add essential oils as well.

Example

$\frac{1}{3}$ cup calendula oil

$\frac{1}{3}$ cup St. John's wort oil

$\frac{1}{3}$ cup plantain oil
$\frac{1}{4}$ cup beeswax

Just before you pour into the jars, add 10 drops of lavender essential oil.
   This salve is excellent for diaper rash, cuts, abrasions and bruises, chapped skin, burns and bug bites.

Anointing oils

These are made by adding essential oils to plain or infused oils for their metaphysical properties. Attention is paid to the lunation when they will be made – a fire oil during a Fire Moon, an earth oil during an Earth Moon, a personal oil during your own Sun or Moon sign, etc. To 1 oz. of carrier oil (I generally use almond oil) add 10–12 drops total of your chosen essential oils.

Trinity oil

At the New Moon, place three sprigs of hyssop and three sprigs of vervain in a small jar and fill with olive oil. Let sit until the Full Moon. Strain and pour into a special bottle. Use sparingly (it is very potent!) to draw good fortune, money luck and success.

Solace and comfort oil

Combine the following essential oils in 1 oz. of carrier oil:

Clary sage – 3 drops
Marjoram – 3 drops
Lemon – 3 drops
Spikenard – 3 drops

Prophetic dream oil

Make when the Moon is in Pisces, ruled by Neptune, the planet of dreams and the subconscious.

Anise – 4 drops
Chamomile – 3 drops
Rose geranium – 3 drops
In 1 oz. carrier oil

See also the 'Lady of Fire' section. There will be more recipes as we go along.

THE ART OF TINCTURING

To make tinctures, we must first understand the word 'menstruum'. Evolving out of the ancient language of Lunar Astrology, it is derived from the Latin word, menstruus, meaning 'monthly' and the root of words like Moon, month, mind, menstruation. This term was applied because of the influence of the Moon and time of the month exerted upon the preparations. Hence, the ancient ones, with one word, pass down the instruction to make our medicines during certain lunar phases. To review:

1. Primarily harvest and make medicines when the Moon is in a Water or Earth sign, the optimum being Cancer and Taurus.
2. Secondarily, make tonic medicines when the Moon is waxing and make 'eliminating' medicines during the waning Moon.

Possible menstruums

Alcohols

Extract certain chemical constituents (i.e. alkaloids) and preserve the medicine.

Vodka is my primary menstruum of choice. 60% alcohol and 40% water, clear, odourless and tasteless, it allows for better sensual perception (taste, smell, colour) of the herbs properties. Otherwise, brandy, whiskey, rum, gin or tequila can be used. Brandy and whiskey make very nice tasting 'toddies' for bronchial complaints.

Many contemporary herbalists use grain alcohol. It is 100 proof and water must be added to the formulation. In my experience, I have not found it to be more effective than other alcohols.

Wines

More anciently used than distilled alcohols, use white wine for the soft parts of plants (leaves and flowers) and red wine for hard parts of plants (seeds, berries, bark and roots). These are taken as tonics, one wine glassful daily.

Apple cider vinegar

Good for tonic, nutrient herbs, apple cider vinegar offers an acidic base for calcium absorption and is appropriate for arthritis and osteoporosis formulas, children and anyone allergic to alcohol. When strained, mix

with honey to make honegar. Honegar is an old Celtic tonic, taken daily to heighten strength and vitality and protect against allergies and infections.

Fresh plant tincture

Harvest the desired plant. If you are working with leaves, simply chop into small pieces. Do NOT wash, as you will wash off essential oils and other constituents. If working with roots, lightly scrub and chop into small pieces. (A little dirt in the jar will not hurt a thing and will be filtered out when you strain it.) Fill a wide mouth mason jar with the processed plant. Next, pour in your desired menstruum until it comes to the very top of the jar. Then take a chopstick or the end of a wooden spoon and poke it down into the jar a few times to release any air bubbles. Top off with additional menstruum, if required. Cap and label with masking tape. (Save your nice labels for the final bottle.) Include the name of the plant, the menstruum used, and the date and the moon phase it was gathered in. Shake well. Place in a warm, dark spot for a full moon cycle, about 28 days. Strain through muslin cloth and bottle. Label and store.

Honegar recipe

Gather fresh, nutrient herbs such as chickweed, cleavers, dandelion, nettles, dock, geranium, mallow and tincture in organic apple cider vinegar for one month. Strain and mix with an equal part of raw honey and store in glass jars or bottles in a dark place. Three times daily, blend 1 tablespoon honegar with 8 oz. water and drink. It is delicious, full of nutrition and refreshing!

Glycerine

This is the sweet principle extracted from certain vegetable oils. It is soothing, preservative, slightly antiseptic and decreases oxidation. For fresh plants, use 80–90% glycerine and 10% water. For dry plant, use a 1 part plant to 4 parts menstruum made from a 60% glycerine and 40% water mix.

Honey

This is anti-microbial, anti-inflammatory, anti-allergenic, mildly sedative, preservative, enzymatic, and high in Vitamin E.

To make honey tinctures, combine 1 part herb with 2 parts honey. Allow to infuse for 2 weeks to 1 month.

WEAVING THE WEB

Suggestions for working with the Spirit of Fire and the lessons of this chapter

Make an altar to honour the Spirit of Fire. Ask that the Fire stay within appropriate boundaries. Contemplate the nature of Fire in your life – is it gentle, intense, overwhelming, non-existent, etc. Brighid can help us to bring Fire into a good balance in our lives.

Make the Brighid's Fire Oil and anoint in different ways, making affirmations as you do. 'Brighid's light is within me, without me and around me', 'Brighid's light is present and prevailing here', etc.

Dedicate a candle to Brighid, anoint it with the oil and light it. Meditate on the gentle light. Breathe it into yourself.

Study the Digestive System notes. Contemplate its relationship with Fire. Try out some of the recipes and/or make your own digestive formula.

Create a blessing to say over your food, if you don't have one already.

Obtain some of the three herbs of the **Materia Medica** *and work with them in as many ways as possible. Record your experiences.*

CHAPTER 4

LADY OF WATER

In Her aspect of Water, Brighid is the Lady of the Healing Spring, Lady of compassion and healing. She turns no one away who is in need and ready to accept Her grace.

From the Book of Lismore

> *Once when Brighid was in Armagh, two persons passed Her, bearing a tub of water. They came to be blessed by Brighid. The tub fell behind them and rolled over and over from the door of the stronghold down to Loch Laphain. But it was not broken, and not a drop fell out. It was manifest to everyone that Brighid's blessing was upon them. Thereafter, Patrick said: 'Deal out the water to Armagh and Airthir'.*
>
> *And every disease and every ailment that was in the land was healed.*

For millennia, the waters that flow from Brighid's wells are reputed to be endowed with the power to heal and transform all manner of disease. These sacred wells are scattered throughout the countryside of England, Wales, Scotland and Ireland. For millennia, women have gathered these sacred waters to use in their healing work, brewing medicine teas and soaking their blue cloths to wash wounds and lay on fevered brows. The gift of a strip of cloth or ribbon is often left tied to the branch of a nearby tree, often a hawthorn, in exchange for the healing. The waters were also sprinkled around dwelling places, gardens and fields, and on livestock for Bride's blessings of protection and abundance.

The only thing Brighid requires for Her healing miracles is that we share the compassion we have received with others as exemplified in this story:

> *And so it was that Brighid received the gift of a milk cow and she gave it away to a man who was destitute. The story was told around the county until it came to the ears of two men who suffered from leprosy. They undertook a pilgrimage to where Brighid was and when they found Her, they asked Her would she please bless them with the wealth of a cow, that they could experience that state of wealth before they died of the dreadful disease they were suffering from; and Brighid said to them:*
>
> *'Would it not be greater wealth to be healed of your disease?'*
>
> *'Oh, Lady', the man said, 'We would not have dreamed it possible! Oh, yes! Oh, yes!'*
>
> *'Very well then', said Brighid, and taking Her blue cloth and dipping it into a bowl of water, drawn from Her healing*

74

> *springs, She gave it to the first man and bid him bathe the*
> *second man's sores and lesions. Lo! As the man did so, the*
> *sores and lesions disappeared and the second man stood before*
> *him, cured.*
>
> *Then taking up a fresh cloth and bowl of water, Brighid*
> *gave them to the man who had just been cured and said,*
> *'Now do for your brother what he has done for you'.*
>
> *But the man, with his fresh, clean skin, was repulsed and*
> *he refused, for he lacked faith in the Lady's miracles and he*
> *only cared to preserve his new health.*
>
> *Brighid took the cloth and water and began to bathe the*
> *sores and lesions of the man who still suffered. Lo! For every*
> *lesion and sore that disappeared on him was returned to the*
> *man who had refused to touch him. Brighid turned to the man*
> *who was once again diseased and said:*
>
> *'And so shall you remain – until you learn*
> *compassion.'*

Brighid can turn the water into wine and milk, quenching the thirst of the multitudes. She was renowned for the beer She brewed and passed this art on to Her priestesses who passed it on to the village women.

Her generosity knows no bounds. All that She is given by the rich, She turns and gives to the poor. As a child, She was always giving away Her father's possessions to those in need. As She grew up, She served for a time as a shepherdess and dairy-maid on the farm of a Druid.

From the Book of Lismore

> *... A dairy-maid, sweet, gentle, and beautiful, with a*
> *disposition that was perpetual sunshine in her clean, white*
> *dairy, or in the woods with her sheep. In these days Bridget's*
> *heart went out to all living things, to God's beasts and birds*
> *as well as (His) mankind – on all which she lavished her*
> *love. And all in return loved her. Everything to which her*
> *hand was set used to increase. She tended the sheep; she*
> *satisfied the birds; she fed the poor.*

She blesses our hearths and homes with abundance. She is the Divine Midwife, present at every birth and every death; She is the Virgin Mother, blessing women and the herd with fertility. Her ever-flowing compassion and love are inherent in the waters of natural springs and rivers.

A Water Blessing: the Prayer of the Chalice

(Said before drinking a glass of spring water)

> *Mother, to Thee I raise my whole being,*
> *A vessel emptied of self.*
> *Accept, Lady, this my emptiness,*
> *And so fill me with Thyself –*
> *Thy light, Thy love, Thy life –*
> *That these precious gifts*
> *May radiate through me*
> *And overflow the chalice of my heart*
> *Into the hearts of all with whom*
> *I come in contact this day, revealing unto them*
> *The beauty of Thy joy and Wholeness*
> *And the serenity of Thy Peace*
> *Which nothing can destroy.*

One day, seven holy men came to visit Brighid and She was appalled that She had no food for them, for She was renowned for Her generous hospitality. She prayed and angels told Her the cows would give milk for the third time that day. Brighid milked the cows Herself and they gave abundantly and all the containers of Leinster were filled.

THE HEALING POWER OF BRIGHID'S WATERS

Like fire, water was recognized as precious and sacred by our ancestors. We can participate in restoring its sacredness by acknowledging its healing and nourishing powers. We can perceive our tap water to be as holy as water from the healing wells, nourishing the spirit with our honour and appreciation.

While the opportunity to gather water from one of Brighid's acknowledged healing springs is a wonderful thing, it is not always possible. Therefore, we must come to see the sacred in the mundane. There are many ways to resanctify even tap water, for example.

To make Moon Water

On the night of the full Moon, take a beautiful bowl and fill it with water. Take it outside and set it where the moonbeams can infuse it. Bring it inside in the morning before the Sun shines on it. This water can then be used as you would a flower essence to infuse your home

and your person with the Moon's magic, bringing good fortune and fertility, understanding and easy flow of cycles, greater perception of the
mysteries and the power to work with them wisely.

Drinking and bathing with these lunar waters before ritual will
enhance psychic abilities. Use sparingly, as they are potent – 4 drops in
a glass of water for drinking, about 20 drops in a bath for bathing, 10
drops in a quart of water to sprinkle around the home. Store in a glass
bottle in a dark place.

When crafting your lunar waters, the following traditional Gaillic
chant may be spoken; or simply speak from your heart to Brighid in
Her aspect as Mother Moon.

> *Hail to thee, oh Moon*
> *Beauteous guidant of the sky ...*
> *Beauteous fair one of grace ...*
> *Beauteous guidant of the stars ...*
> *Beauteous loved one of my heart ...*
> *Beauteous guidant of the clouds ...*
> *Beauteous dear one of the skies ...*

Hail to thee, Jewel of the Night
Beauty of the skies, Jewel of the Night
Mother of the stars, Jewel of the Night
Foster-child of the Sun, Jewel of the Night
Majesty of the Stars, Jewel of the Night.

Failt ort fhein, a gealeach
Ailleagan iuil nan speur
Ailleagan fionn na feil
Ailleagan iuil nan reul
Ailleagan ruin mo chleibh
Ailleagan iuil nan neul
Ailleagan cumh nan neamh

Failt dhuit fhein, Eiteag na h-oidhche
Ailleachd nan speur, Erteag na h-oidhche
Mathair nan reul, Eiteag na h-oidhche
Dalta na greine, Eiteag na h-oidhche
Morachd nan reul, Eiteag na h-oidhche

Solar waters

On a warm, sunny day, take a beautiful vessel and fill it with water. Place it outside where the Sun's rays will infuse it, then bring it inside and decant it into a bottle. Use in rituals for the attributes of the Sun; worldly success, self-confidence and self-esteem, prosperity, fulfilment of destiny.

Colour waters

These are solar-infused waters taken one step further, developed with the invention of glass. Water is placed in a glass container that is the colour of the energy you are seeking:

Red – energy, connection to life, passion, assertiveness, action, survival.
Orange – creativity, initiative, stimulation, adaptability.
Yellow – self-esteem, confidence, intellect, attraction, persuasion.
Green – fertility, growth, healing, prosperity, money, employment.
Light blue – tranquillity, healing, patience, happiness, communication.
Dark blue – psychism, intuition, the subconscious vision, imagination.
Purple – power, spirituality, meditation, healing severe diseases.

As Lady of the Waters, Brighid will cool and heal fevers and burns and other inflammations. The following is a traditional Cornish invocation to the Triple Brighid against a burn:

> *Three ladies came from the East,*
> *One with fire and two with frost.*
> *Out with thee, fire!*
> *In with thee, frost!*

THE ELEMENT OF WATER

Time – twilight, autumn.

Place – the oceans, womb and heart of Mother Earth, rivers, lakes, pools, streams.

Powers and blessings – emotions, love, courage, daring, sorrow, intuition, the unconscious, dreaming, fertility.

Body systems – the womb, reproductive organs, the heart and circulatory system, the urinary system, birthing.

Deities – Danu, Brighid, Shannon, Boann, Dagda, Mananaan mac Lir.

Spirits – merwomen and mermen, selkies, undines.

Planets and signs – Cancer, Scorpio, Pisces, the Moon, Neptune, Pluto.

Colours – blue, blue-green, sea green, indigo, black, silver.

Animals – sea serpents, water dragons, dolphins and porpoises, fish, seals, whales, sea mammals, sea birds, frogs and toads, all water-dwelling creatures.

Plants – ferns, lotus, mosses, rushes, seaweed, rose, motherwort, marjoram, bleeding heart, violets, rose geranium, elder, willow, alder.

Stones – pearls, aquamarine, rose quartz, chryssacolla, river rocks.

Tools – the chalice or cup, the cauldron, the mirror, shells.

Offerings – waters (flower essences, gem elixirs, colour waters, etc.), wine, teas.

The ritual bath

To ritualize the bath, incorporate the Four Elements. Beautiful music and scents invoke Air, candles invoke Fire, the water in the bath and a delicious glass of something invoke Water, and the herbs (and perhaps some chocolate?) and your body are the Earth.

Bath tea

Make a very strong tea of rosemary, lavender, or any other aromatic herbs you like. Be sure to keep covered while steeping (30 minutes). Strain and add a cup or so to your bath.

Herb bags

Fill muslin bags with a mixture of oatmeal, lavender, rosemary, etc., and use as a body scrubber.

Body scrub

$\frac{1}{2}$ cup bentonite clay.
$\frac{1}{2}$ cup oat flour.
1 cup cornmeal.
Enough honey to make a paste.
Your favourite essential oils – lavender, peppermint, sage, etc.
Mix and spoon into a jar – keep excess refrigerated.

The following recipe may be made as a bath tea or muslin bag scrubber.

Woman of the House bath

Calendula flowers – for respect and admiration.
Dandelion flowers – for clairvoyance and esteem.
Lemon verbena leaves – for poise and confidence.
Anise seed – to stimulate the mind and body, psychic power.
Rosemary – for respect and dominion in the house.
Rose geranium leaves and flowers – for beauty and sensuality.

Elemental baths

Add essential oils to $\frac{1}{2}$ cup of sea salt.

Air

For renewal, mental energy, to shift patterns of thinking.
3 drops lavender
2 drops rosemary
2 drops chamomile
2 drops clary sage
Colour: light blue

Fire

To increase passion, vitality, self-esteem; to empower action.
3 drops basil
2 drops lemon
3 drops amber
1 drop ginger
Colour: yellow

Water

To soothe, heal, deepen; to open and heal the heart.
3 drops rose geranium
2 drops ylang ylang
2 drops mugwort
Colour: deep blue

Earth

To ground, centre, and magnetise prosperity.
3 drops oak moss
2 drops spikenard
2 drops vetivert
1 drop sage
Colour: green

Airmid's bath of renewal

3 drops angelica
2 drops rosemary
2 drops frankincense

This can also be translated into the bath bag using whole herbs – try to get powdered frankincense, as it is a very hard resin. Drops become parts, therefore 3 drops=3 parts.

High awareness bath

3 drops clary sage
2 drops frankincense
2 drops peppermint

Sweet sleep bath

Make a strong cup of chamomile tea. To the strained tea, add 3 table-spoons of honey and 5 drops of lavender essential oil. Pour slowly into the bath water and soak for 10 to 15 minutes.

THE ART OF FLOWER ESSENCES

Flower essences are infused with the spirit of the plant and affect the emotional, mental and ethereal bodies, ultimately affecting the physical. Flower waters have, I'm sure, been made from the beginning of time.

Dr. Bach (1886–1936) perfected the art when he left his medical practice in London and sold all his material goods, except for one suitcase filled with his precious books, which he would carry with him, and a suitcase full of old shoes, which he planned to drop off at a homeless shelter on his way out of the city. He had decided that he needed to get out into the countryside and learn from the plants themselves. He walked out of London, dropping one of the suitcases off as he left. Travelling for some time, through fields and meadows and over hills, he finally sat down under an oak tree to rest his feet and decided he'd have a look at his books while he was sitting there. Well, what do you think? He opened the suitcase and there were all his old shoes! He had left the 'wrong' suitcase at the shelter! Except it turned out that it was exactly the right one, for as the gentle doctor discovered, he wore out every pair of those shoes walking around the countryside and not having his books encouraged his psychic relationship with the plants. And so we are reminded to get our heads out of the books and go learn from the plants themselves!

In his book, *Heal Thyself*, written in 1931, Dr. Bach wrote 'The action of these (flower) remedies is to raise our vibrations and open up our channels for the reception of the Spiritual Self, to flood our natures with the particular virtue we need, and wash from us the fault that is causing the harm. They are able, like beautiful music or any glorious uplifting thing which gives us inspiration, to raise our very natures, and bring us nearer to our souls and by that very act to bring us peace and relieve our sufferings. They cure, not by attacking the disease, but by flooding our bodies with the beautiful vibrations of our Higher Nature, in the presence of which, disease melts away as snow in the sunshine'.

Flower essences help us to transform the negative energy patterns that are the result of our ego's illusions of isolation, resulting in physical patterns of disease. They help to eliminate the fear, anger, doubt, confusion, etc. that separates us from our true selves.

As I think you will agree, once you have made and used them yourself, flower essences beautifully prove the healing powers of gentleness and simplicity, and that healing the heart heals the body. They are ecologically sound, as only a few flowers are required to make many bottles of essence.

MAKING THE FLOWER ESSENCES

On a bright, sunny day, fill a small, clear glass or crystal vessel with spring water. Let your vessel be pretty that it may do honour to the flower's beauty and consider the size of the flower in proportion to the size of the vessel. If you're making thyme essence, for example, and you choose a large bowl for your vessel, you're going to be there a very long time gathering enough of the tiny flowers to cover the whole surface!

Take the water to the plant you'd like to work with as well as a note-book to record your 'impressions'. Greet the plant and take note of the surroundings from the hawk and butterfly view.

Next, close your eyes, allow yourself to relax deeply and visualise the spirit of the plant coming forth and sprinkling a magic dust on you, which allows you to grow as small as a bee. Fly up to the flower and sit on the petal. Look out and see the world as the plant does. Notice the colours, patterns and scent of the flower. Next, find the entrance to the stalk of the flower and, allowing yourself to become smaller still, enter and find yourself flowing in a green, green river of chlorophyll. Flow down the stalk and off into the 'estuary' veins of the leaves, back out into the green river, flowing down, down into the roots of the plant. Notice the changes of colour, light, energy, feel the Earth and, when you are ready, allow yourself to begin flowing back up through the stalk, in the green chlorophyll river. Allow yourself to be 'washed' and energised by the chlorophyll, noticing what emotions surface and transform. Flow up and up until you are once again resting on the petal of the flower. Here, let the spirit of the plant give you any more information that you are to receive at this time. This can come in words, pictures, feelings and other sensings. You may experience 'nega-tive' emotions – these are the emotions this plant can heal. Thank the spirit of the plant and return to your body. Record your sensings.

Now it is time to gather the flowers. Using a leaf or twigs, without touching the flowers yourself, gently pull the flowers off the plant and place them on the surface of the water. Leave the vessel to sit by the 'mother' plant for three hours under the Sun. Then, remove the flowers, once again using a leaf or twigs and place around the plant. Gift the plant. The water you now hold is called the 'mother essence'.

Next, you will make stock bottles. It is from the stock bottles that you will make dosage bottles for individual use. When you buy a Bach flower kit, you are buying stock bottles of the essences. I've been making dosage bottles from my kit for 10 years now and I still have plenty left. So you begin to see how a very little goes a very long way.

To make a stock bottle, put two drops of the mother essence into a one-ounce bottle filled with brandy or vodka. This will keep indefinitely and make a multitude of dosage bottles. Now, you will notice that you still have a lot of 'mother' water left. You can make more stock bottles and give them to your friends and/or give the essence back to the plant from which you made it. (I also have fantasies of putting some of that extra stock water into certain water systems.)

Now to make your dosage bottles. I make these up 'in the moment', according to need. Fill a one-ounce dropper bottle with pure water and one teaspoon of brandy or vodka, and then add two drops of each flower essence selected, up to five or six in a combination. Shake well to activate.

How to administer

Take four drops at a time, at least four times a day, directly under the tongue. For maximum effect, hold in the mouth a moment and make an affirmation. To increase the effect, increase the frequency, not the quantity. Flower essences can also be added to creams and lotions, baths, compresses, room sprays and blessing waters.

There are absolutely no harmful side effects, no need to worry about contra-indications and they will work with any other mode of healing.

SOME OF THE GIFTS OF SOME OF THE FLOWERS

It is important to remember that each one of us will have our own unique perspectives of the plants. There are no right or wrongs here, merely layer upon layer of character, strengths and gifts.

The following are some of the flowers and some of their gifts that we have confirmed or newly gathered here at the Academy.

Blackberry – overcoming apathy, inertia; empowers the taking of ideas into action; bestows the will to manifest one's dreams and grow beyond one's limitations. Assists with personal boundaries, especially for those who need to learn to take their full space. Increases tenacity, determination, confidence and energy.

Borage – bestows cheerful courage, confidence in facing danger and challenge, facilitates overcoming depression, discouragement, grief, feelings of heaviness, especially in the heart and chest, feeling disheartened. Also helpful for dispirited animals.

Chamomile – restores calm when emotionally upset; excellent for hyper-activity in children, nervousness and emotional tension in the stomach. Enhances self-expression, openness, tenderness and the willingness to be vulnerable. Helps to heal childhood issues.

Dandelion – greatly enhances self-esteem and the determination to succeed. Increases mental, physical and emotional flexibility and adaptability to life's circumstances. Encourages the release of emotional tension in the body. A great ally during stressful times.

Mallow – heals emotional hurt and reinstates feelings of openness and trust, aiding in overcoming social insecurity and the tendency to withhold in relationships.

Prunella – provides the motivation and confidence to heal from within. For those who doubt their healing abilities and look to others to take responsibility. Helps with emotional addiction, reducing dependence on others.

Red clover – instils calm in the midst of panic and chaos – a good one to keep in the first aid kit. Strengthens unification and solidarity during situations of emergency and intense emotion.

Rose – The ultimate symbol of love! Increases confidence concerning sexuality; heals body shame and timidity. Helps to open to love and bring desire into manifestation.

Scots broom – seeing obstacles as opportunities for growth and service to the world. Especially for the feeling of impending apocalypse which darkens or burdens the psyche; for overcoming pessimism and despair, the feeling of 'what's the use?' when depression is more than merely personal but oriented toward the world situation.

Skullcap – calms the nervous system and heals damage from over-stimulation. Helps with withdrawal symptoms from drugs and other addictions connected with anxiety, low self-esteem and the inability to cope with life. Bestows a sense of physical and mental well being.

Yarrow – for those who are ultra-sensitive to environmental and emotional influences. Strengthens and clarifies boundaries, the aura and the immune system. Cohesifies the Self, enhancing the ability to remain on the path.

THE URINARY SYSTEM

Composed of the kidneys, urethra, ureters and bladder, the urinary system is the 'water treatment plant' of our body.

The main functions of the kidneys

As blood, supplied by the renal arteries, circulates through the kidneys, it is filtered, purified and adjusted. The kidneys void substances the body doesn't need and cleanse the body of wastes and toxins, including sodium chloride, uric acid and nitrogen. Nitrogen is a waste product of protein and can quickly reach toxic levels. The kidneys excrete nitrogen in the form of urea and ammonia.

They balance the body's acid/alkaline nature and the concentration of salts, minerals and other substances.

The kidneys collect chemicals and fluids, including glucose and amino acids, water, and other positive ions, from the blood flow and regulate levels of chloride, sodium, potassium and bicarbonate. (In diabetes, glucose is not reabsorbed.)

They regulate the proper balance between body and water content and salt, retaining water or salt depending on requirements.

They form urine and adjust the output to equal the intake of water.

Once the blood is filtered, urine is produced containing the unwanted substances. The urine is stored in the bladder until evacuation.

The kidneys are responsible for blood pressure. Without them our hearts could not beat.

They contribute to homeostasis by governing water, chemical and acid balance.

The function of the urinary system

The urinary system filters waste products from the body via a system of tubes. Blood is filtered in the two fist-sized, bean-shaped kidneys, located directly behind the lower ribs, tucked in the upper abdomen. The right kidney is about half an inch lower than the left to accommodate the liver. There is a heavy cushion of fat around them for protection.

Renal arteries carry blood to the kidneys where the kidneys collect fluid and chemicals. The kidneys have first priority, with the heart and brain, for blood supply, as their job must continue, even if it means stressing other organs.

Renal veins carry blood away after filtering after filtering chemicals to be reabsorbed and those passed as urine.

Each kidney contains 1 million micro-funnels called nephrons. Each nephron is made up of a renal tubule, where water and nutrients are reabsorbed into the blood, and a filtering unit called a glomerulus, consisting of a ball of tiny blood vessels. The blood vessel coming into the glomerulus is larger than the one leaving, creating blood pressure. A hollow Bowman's capsule surrounds each glomerulus.

This combined unit (the glomerulus and Bowman's capsule) is called the renal corpuscle.

Urine is carried from the kidneys to the bladder by two ureters. The ureters are tubes $\frac{1}{4}$ inch wide and about 12 inches long, descending from the kidneys to the bladder. They have muscular walls for peristalsis-like action.

If a lot of water is lost, for example when sweating, less is excreted in the urine.

Large amounts of water taken in will correspond to higher urine output.

In cold weather, urine output is more abundant, due to less perspiration.

Urine is sterile at the moment it leaves the body, then quickly becomes susceptible to bacteria.

When dehydration threatens, the kidneys continue to draw water from other tissues to produce urine.

Urine is coloured by a pigment called urochrome. When kidneys excrete large amounts of water, urine is dilute, clear to pale yellow in colour and initially odourless.

When the body needs to conserve liquid, e.g. during sleep, the kidneys produce darker, more concentrated urine. It is always a signal to give the body more water! One of the more ancient forms of diagnosis, definitely easier in the days of bedpans, was examination of the patient's urine, with the colour and odour communicating various things, from dehydration to the presence of infection.

The kidneys are 'the seat of our emotions'. They hold feelings, especially fear and loneliness, and absorb shock and trauma. Keep them warm, protected and well-watered!

Positive thinking and exercise also help to keep them working efficiently.

Symptoms of imbalance

1. Dark, puffy circles under the eyes
2. Pre-menstrual stress
3. Itchy eyes
4. Lower back pain – tenderness near the kidneys
5. Water retention
6. Allergies/hay fever
7. High blood pressure
8. Low blood pressure
9. Ear and eye irritation
10. Depression/moodiness
11. Restlessness/insomnia
12. Skin rashes

URINARY SYSTEM *MATERIA MEDICA*

Tonics: help maintain the integrity of the kidneys. Agrimony, dandelion leaf, borage, chickweed, cleavers, cornsilk, cinnamon, parsley, mallow, plantain, rosehips, saw palmetto, violet leaf, yarrow. Water, water, water!

Demulcents: keep the system moisturised. Borage, cornsilk, cinnamon, mallow, marshmallow, parsley, plantain.

Astringents: strengthen and tone the tissues. Cleavers, horsetail (use short term), parsley, plantain, yarrow.

Diuretics: encourage flushing and correct water retention. Chickweed, cleavers, cornsilk, celery seed, chamomile, dandelion leaf, lovage, meadowsweet, nasturtium, plantain, parsley, juniper berries, wild carrot.

Anti-microbials: to treat infections of the urinary tract. Celery seed, chamomile, lovage, juniper berries, meadowsweet, plantain, nasturtium, parsley, rosehips, thyme.

Anti-spasmodics: help relieve pain and spasms. Chamomile, crampbark, juniper, parsley, plantain, wild carrot.

Anti-inflammatories: chamomile, cleavers, juniper, plantain, thyme.

Anti-lithics: dissolve stones in the urinary tract. Chamomile, cleavers, lovage, parsley, wild carrot.

Lymphatics: support the 'other' filtering system, taking pressure off the kidneys. Cleavers, calendula, water, laughter, exercise, massage.

Chologogues/hepatics: support elimination through the liver and gall bladder. Agrimony, chamomile, dandelion root, dock, yarrow.

Nervines: to shift negative emotions. Chamomile, motherwort, borage, lemon balm, vervain, aromatherapy.

URINARY TRACT INFECTIONS

Urinary tract infections or UTI are bacterial infections of some part of the urinary tract. There are three types of urinary tract infection.

1. *Cystitis*: the most common. Infection of the bladder.
2. *Pylonephritis*: infection of the kidney – this is serious!
3. *Urethritis*: infection of the urethra.

More common in females than males, contamination can occur from contact with stool during wiping or as a secondary infection from bacteria in the vaginal tract. In older males, infections are commonly a complication of an enlarged prostate.

Common symptoms of cystitis or urethritis include painful urination, increased and urgency of urination, low back pain and low grade fever.

Common symptoms of pylonephritis include high fever, chills, vomiting and pain in the small of the back.

Therapies

A possible formula

Urinary tonic – dandelion leaf – 2 oz.
Anti-microbial – thyme – 2 oz.
Anti-inflammatory – thyme
Demulcent – marshmallow root – 1 oz.
Febrifuge – yarrow – 1 oz.
Antispasmodic – 2 oz.

Infuse $\frac{1}{4}$ cup of the above mixture in 1 quart of water. Drink 4–6 cups a day for two weeks.

Additional therapies

Drink lots of water
Go to bed

Have a good cry (remember the 'seat of emotions'? I have seen most cases of cystitis 'turn the corner' after this has occurred.)

Take baths with $\frac{1}{2}$ cup sea salt and $\frac{1}{2}$ cup apple cider vinegar to draw out infection. Essential oils can be added such as lavender, juniper or myrrh.

Avoid alcohol, sugar, spices and caffeine. Fast on veggies, broths and juices, potatoes.

WEAVING THE WEB

Suggestions for working with the Spirit of Fire and the lessons of this chapter

Make an altar to honour the Spirit of Fire. Ask that the Fire stay within appropriate boundaries. Contemplate the nature of Fire in your life – is it gentle, intense, overwhelming, non-existent, etc. Brighid can help us to bring Fire into a good balance in our lives.

Make the Brighid's Fire Oil and anoint in different ways, making affirmations as you do. 'Brighid's light is within me, without me and around me', 'Brighid's light is present and prevailing here', etc.

Dedicate a candle to Brighid, anoint it with the oil and light it. Meditate on the gentle light. Breathe it into yourself.

Study the Digestive System notes. Contemplate its relationship with fire. Try out some of the recipes and/or make your own digestive formula.

Create a blessing to say over your food, if you don't have one already.

Obtain some of the three herbs of the Materia Medica *and work with them in as many ways as possible. Record your experiences.*

Make at least one flower essence. Take it every day for one week. How does it effect your emotions?

Make some tinctures. Experiment with menstruums. Don't be afraid to make mistakes, they are the best teachers.

Do your emotions flow or do they tend to get dammed up and stuck? Work with the above to help them move.

Visit a body of water. A river, a spring, a lake an ocean. Make an offering. Sit and listen to the water's wisdom.

Make a ritual bath for your self. Steep in the blessings of the plants. Add some sea salt to re-create the primordial womb of the Mother and be reborn.

CHAPTER 5

LADY OF EARTH

As a Lady of Earth, Brighid is a very real woman of flesh and blood and bone, gifted in the arts of brewing ale, the baking of bread, the keeping of the henhouse and dairy house, farming and homemaking, spinning, weaving, the gathering of herbs and crafting of remedies, and the healing of physical ailments. Her best known earthly incarnation is that of St. Brigid of Kildare, d. 525, who embodied all of those qualities and more.

Brighid is the guardian of the pastoral folk who work the land. She protects the harvest and the home, be it humble croft or grand palace. She increases the yield of cow and sheep and anything She sets Her hand to.

From the Book of Lismore

Lassair said to Brighid:
'What shall we do for the multitude of people that have come to us?'
'What food do we have?' asked Brighid.
'We have nothing except one sheep, twelve loaves and a little milk,' answered Lassair.
'Well enough,' Brighid said. 'We will have abundance and all will be fed generously.'
The food was brought to Her and She prayed over it and blessed it.
And the multitude was fed their fill and there was more food left over than they started with.

As a woman of Earth, Brighid exemplifies the sacredness of the mundane, reminding us that the activities of the hearth and home are the core, the heart of life. Whatever is nourished in the home is taken out into the world, impacting culture and ecology. If selfishness, disrespect, violence, and other negativities are practised in the home, these are the energies that will flow out into the world. If love and peace, generosity, respect, and other positive energies are nourished, then that home will be a sacred sanctuary, creating more sacred space; and the energies that flow from it shall be a blessing to the world. Any and all of us can take the power to create harmony in our dwelling places, thereby contributing to the Greater Harmony.

A HOUSE BLESSING TO WELCOME BRIGHID

1. Open all windows and doors to let the old out and the new in. Take off shoes at the door to leave the world outside.
2. Sweep or vacuum the whole house.
3. Wash down the walls and floors with one cup of vervain tea and one cup of vinegar stirred into a gallon of water.
4. Light incense and walk it around the house, through all the rooms, or pass around the circle and mentally spread through the house.
   House of Harmony incense:
   > 2 parts vervain – for sacredness, prosperity, protection.
   > 1 part wormwood – for peace.
   > 1 part rosemary – for respect and good communication.
   > 1 part lavender – for clarity and delight.
   > 1 part sage – for wisdom and groundedness.
   > 1 part lady's mantle – Brighid's Cloak of Protection.
5. Anoint a candle and yourselves with Trinity Oil:
   > one pinch of vervain.
   > one pinch of hyssop.
   > infused into one ounce of olive oil.

   Light a candle and walk it around the house, or pass it around the circle, chanting:
   > Cuiram air an Lampa de Bhride
   > (We kindle the Light of Bride)
6. Now sprinkle a blessing water around the house or circle. Sing or say to the Spirit of the Home:
   > Deep peace of the running wave to you.
   > Deep peace of the flowing air to you.
   > Deep peace of the quiet Earth to you.

Moon and Stars pour their healing light on you.
Deep peace, deep peace.

7. If this is a blessing for a house that is just being moved into, carry in:
   - a chair to represent comfort and rest,
   - a bowl of salt for protected boundaries,
   - a loaf of bread for harmony, nourishment, and plenty,
   - a bottle of red wine or mead for love, health, and life force.

Otherwise, have these offerings present at the feasting table. For a new home, the meal should be potluck, brought by the guests. If a private house blessing, prepare a meal ahead of time, consisting of your favourite foods.

Now that you have prepared your home, it is time to go to the door and invite Brighid to come in and reside there.

The woman chosen to represent Brighid now goes outside and gathers a bunch of rushes, then returns and calls out:

> *Téigi ar bhur nglúine, agus osclaigi bhur súile,*
> *Agus ligigi Bríd bheannaithe isteach!*
>
> *(Be on your knees, and open your eyes,*
> *And let blessed Brid in!)*

The participants in the blessing respond:

> *Sé do bheatha, sé do bheatha,*
> *Sé do bheatha, a bhean uasail!*
>
> *Welcome home, welcome home!*
> *Welcome home, blessed woman!*
>
> *O, tar isteach,*
> *Tá caed failte romhat!*
>
> *O, come in,*
> *You are a hundred times welcome!*

The woman representing Brighid now enters the house and lays the rushes under the table and blesses the house and all in it, particularly the food and drink, and the hearthfire (or stove, if there is no fireplace).

The household and guests may now make crasóga, Brighid's crosses, from the rushes, which are then hung up over doors and windows to protect from want.

Finally, it is time for feasting and (in some cases) the presentation of gifts for the home; gifts that symbolise a blessing a giver would like to make to the home, such as plants, stones, candles, art, food.

May Brighid bless the house
Wherein you dwell;
Bless every fireside,
Every wall and door;
Bless every heart
That beats beneath its roof;
Bless every hand
That toils to bring it joy;
Bless every foot
That walks its portals through –
May Brighid bless the house that shelters you.
(Traditional)

A TRADITIONAL TURNIP SOUP RECIPE

(You could serve this at your House Blessing)

Originally cooked in a bastable, a three-legged iron pot with a lid that could be suspended over the fire, commonly used in every household for the making of soups, stews, pot roasts, and breads.

Ingredients

    3 large turnips
    1 large onion
    1 pint of milk
    $1\frac{1}{2}$ pints of chicken stock
    2 ounces of butter
    1 ounce of flour
    1 teaspoon of honey
    salt and pepper (to taste)
    a pinch of thyme

Preparation

Peel and chop the turnips and onion; add to melted butter in a saucepan, cover closely and cook gently for 20 minutes. Then add the stock and thyme and simmer for 30 minutes or until the turnip is tender. Rub through a sieve and return to the pan. Mix the flour to a smooth paste with a little of the milk, then add to the soup with the rest of the milk, and the honey. Season to taste and cook for 10 minutes.

BRIGHID CAKES

Ingredients

> 9 ounces of whole wheat flour
> 2 ounces of honey
> 6 ounces of butter
> A good handful of hazelnuts

Preparation

Cream together the honey and butter. Add flour and hazelnuts. Flatten dough to $\frac{1}{2}$-inch thickness. Cut or shape into crescents and sunwheels. Bake at 300 °F until golden (about 15–20 minutes).

HEALING SPELLS

The Charm of the Sprain

(Said while laying hands on the wound)
> *Bride went out*
> *In the morning early*
> *With a pair of horses.*
> *One broke his leg.*
> *With much ado,*
> *That was apart,*
> *She put bone to bone,*
> *She put flesh to flesh,*
> *She put sinew to sinew,*
> *She put vein to vein.*
> *As She healed that,*
> *May I heal this.*

The Assumption of the Oak

Take the used bandages from the wound and dress with rue oil. Bury them at the foot of an oak tree and allow the tree to transform the wound to wholeness.

Or...

Rub an apple or an egg over the diseased area, then bury as before.

HOW BRIGHID OBTAINED HER LAND

As Brighid's flocks of sheep and students began to grow, She realised She would need more land to house them. Taking four of Her aid-women with Her, She approached the chieftain of Leinster Ailill, and asked him if he would deed a piece of land to Her. The Chieftain laughed and said, 'Sure, I'll give you as much land as your cloak will cover!' And Brighid and Her aid-women and all the folk of the village trooped out to the curragh and with everyone looking on Brighid had Her four aid-women each take a corner of Her cloak, one walking toward the East, one walking toward the South, one walking toward the West, and one toward the North – and what do you know? Brighid's cloak began to grow and grow and grow until it covered the whole of the curragh!

The Chieftain Ailill was so astounded by this miracle happening right before his eyes and he deeded the land to Brighid right then and there. And for the rest of his life, he abided by Her counsel.

Brighid built Her sanctuary and school by a great oak tree and no one was allowed to put a plough to the land that became known as 'Brighid's Pastures'.

WAYS TO HONOUR BRIGHID AND HER ASPECT OF EARTH

1. Give to the poor – feed someone who's hungry.
2. Offer hospitality to travellers.
3. Plant trees, herbs, and flowers. Plant a vegetable garden for the homeless.
4. Take care of the Earth – recycle, clean up litter, conserve and preserve.
5. Cook a wonderful meal and invite people to share it.
6. Make your home a sanctuary – a clean and comfortable place for Brighid's Light to dwell in.
7. Make a ritual of gratitude to the Land for all She gives us. Offer gifts of Air, Fire, Water, and Earth.

ELEMENTS OF EARTH

Time – midnight, dark moon, winter.
Place – the north, mountains, caves, groves, fields.

Powers and blessings – abundance, completion, boundaries, sustenance, practicality, sensuality, harvest, fruition, experience, releasing, composting, manifesting, birth, death, ancestors, herbs, touch, massage, chiropracty, sculpture.

Body systems – muscle, skeleton, skin, breasts, vulva, reproductive.

Deities – Eriu, Brighid, Ceres, Demeter, Mother Earth, Nerthus, the Crone, Tara, Dagda, Cernunnos, the Green Man, Robin Hood, Merlin.

Planets and signs – Saturn, Virgo, Taurus, Capricorn.

Colours – white of snow, black of midnight, green of plants, brown of soil, grey of rocks.

Animals – deer, bull and cow, sheep, goat, pig, boar, beaver, bear, serpent.

Plants – comfrey, vervain, oak leaves, acorns, sage, ladies mantle, mint, blackberry, nettles, grains, roots.

Spirits – gnomes, elves, trolls.

Stones – obsidian, smoky quartz, moss agate, fossils, rocks.

Tools – stones, bones, pottery, food, amulets, jewels, gem elixirs.

Offerings – fruit, grains, roots, salt, stones, clay.

Earth incense

Make when the moon is in the sign of Taurus. Use in rituals for matters of the physical plane – money, health, home, work, grounding, etc.

> Comfrey leaf 1 pt
> Vervain 2 pts.
> Mint 2 pts.
> Sage 1 pt.
> Oak leaves 1 pt.

THE POWER OF STONES

Agate – Grounding, acceptance, security, harmony.

Amber – Actually a fossilised resin, known as 'the Mother Stone', bestows confidence, deepening, connection to ancestors and history, calming, soothing, protection.

Amethyst – Develops intuition in a grounded way. Brain tonic, uplifting, balancing, mental focus.

Carnelian – Strength and stamina, dispels depression, creativity, grounded fire.

Clear quartz – Amplifies, transmits, promotes clarity, connection to the Higher Self.

Fluorite – Clears mental and psychic clutter. Ally for computer users.

Fossils – The history keepers. Attunement with the ancestors and other ages.

Garnet – Body strength, endurance, vitality, self-esteem, will power. The power of the Crone.

Haematite – The blood of Mother Earth. Grounding and stabilising. Heals blood disorders. Protection.

Malachite – Intensifies moods, positive or negative. Stirs up old or suppressed negative emotions so they may be released. Aids mental balance, releases toxins and then protects against them. Aids processing in the dreamstate.

Moonstone – Balances emotions. Facilitates relationship to the Feminine. Receptivity, sensitivity, intuition, psychic powers, the Moon.

Obsidian – The Master Teacher. Absorbs negativity and transforms it into light. Aids prophetic vision, the 'magic mirror', grounding and centring in the midst of chaos. Protector of sensitive people, 'disarms' abusers.

Opal – Enhances cosmic consciousness, psychic abilities, emotional balance, and harmony.

Rose quartz – The Heart Stone. Self and universal love. Heals the wounded heart, cynicism and bitterness. Forgiveness. Aligns mental, emotional and spiritual bodies. Increases confidence and creativity.

Rutilated quartz – Moves stuck energy and old patterns. Strengthens immune system and aids tissue regeneration. Facilitates new beginnings.

Smoky quartz – Grounding, balancing and strengthening. Promotes attunement to the physical body and the Earthly realm.

Sodalite – Strengthens and opens the Third Eye. Clear vision and insight. Heals subconscious fear and guilt. Can be used in place of lapis lazuli.

Stones may be incorporated into our lives as amulets, jewellery, meditation tools, and stone elixirs.

TO MAKE A GEM ELIXER

On a sunny day, during an appropriate Moon phase, set your chosen stone in a clear vessel of spring water. Set outside under the Sun's rays for three hours. Strain this 'gem water' without touching it and add $\frac{1}{4}$ cup vodka, whiskey or brandy for every cup of water. Pour into sterilised bottles. Take as you would a flower essence, 4 drops 3–4 times a day. Also, add to the bath, lotions, creams and the ritual cup. I add drops to my indoor fountain and sprinkle around my house to spread their energies.

About Moon phases

Stones are basically Earth with a secondary element usually determined and symbolised by the colour. So I might choose a Fire Moon to make a carnelian gem elixir or an Air Moon to make an amethyst elixir. For Moonstone, I might set it out under a Full Moon, rather than the Sun. As always, let the stones speak to you and follow your intuition!

HOUSEHOLD RECIPES

Floor and wall wash

> 1 gallon of water.
> 1 cup white vinegar.
> 1 cup vervain tea.
> 10 drops lemon essential oil.
> 10 drops thyme essential oil.
> 10 drops lavender essential oil.

To disinfect, purify and bless the home environment.

Natural carpet freshener

1 cup cornstarch (if flea-infested, add 1 oz. powdered rue or pennyroyal).
$\frac{1}{2}$ cup salt.
20 drops total of your favourite essential oil blends.

This will neutralise bacteria, dispel negativity and bless with the intended energies.

Air freshener and disinfectant

In a 12 oz. spray bottle, combine 5 drops lemon, 5 drops peppermint and 10 drops of thyme with water.

Spray periodically to disinfect and clear the air, use to clean countertops and sponges.

Also try substituting peppermint with rosemary, orange, clary sage or lavender. Add ginger or cinnamon in the winter to 'warm' the air.

Moth-repellent sachets

In a cotton muslin bag, combine 6 oz. dry insect-repelling herbs – lavender, wormwood, tansy, rue, southernwood, pennyroyal.

Add $\frac{1}{2}$ oz. orrisroot powder and $\frac{1}{2}$ oz. sweet spice, e.g. cloves, cinnamon.

CULINARY HERBAL DELIGHTS

Food shakes

Sweet treat

Digestive aid – sprinkle on squash, cereals, rice, cookie dough, baked fruit or add to hot apple cider.

  1 pt. cinnamon
  1 pt. coriander
  1 pt. nutmeg
  1 pt. allspice
  1 pt. ginger
  1 pt. stevia

La Fiesta Latina

Circulatory stimulant/immune tonic – sprinkle on rice, popcorn, pasta, veggies, meats.

  1 pt. cumin
  1 pt. paprika
  1 pt. cayenne
  1 pt. garlic
  1 pt. onion
  1 pt. oregano
  1 pt. thyme

Va Bene Italiana

Circulatory stimulant/immune tonic – sprinkle on rice, popcorn, pasta, veggies, meats.

  1 pt. onion
  2 pts. garlic

1 pt. marjoram
1 pt. basil
1 pt. rosemary
1 pt. celery seed

Orient Express

1 pt. sesame seed
1 pt. red/green bell peppers (dry)
1 pt. garlic
1 pt. celery seed

THE SKIN

The skin is one of the largest and most important organs of the body. One of the main immune system interfacers between the environment and ourselves, it is an expression of internal and external factors.

Truly a marvel, the skin contains *within each square inch*: 500 sweat glands, over 1000 nerve endings, yards of tiny blood vessels, about 100 sebaceous glands, 150 sensors for pressure, 75 for heat, 10 for cold and millions of cells!

Skin is structured in two primary layers, the epidermis and the dermis.

The epidermis is the outermost and thinnest primary layer, composed of several layers of stratified squamous epithelium. The innermost layer of cells comprising these tissues continually reproduces and new cells move towards the surface. As these cells approach the surface, they are filled with a tough, waterproof protein called keratin and eventually flake off. (90% of the dust in our homes is dead skin cells.) These outermost layers of keratin-filled cells are called the *stratum corneum*. They 'flake off' by the thousands and millions of epithelial cells reproduce daily to replace the millions shed.

The pigment layer within the epidermis contains pigment cells called melanocytes, which produce the brown pigment melanin.

The dermis is the deeper and thicker of the two primary skin layers and is composed of connective tissue. The upper area of dermis is characterised by parallel rows of peglike dermal papillae, which help to bind the skin layers together at the dermal/epidermal junction. These dermal papillae form our fingerprints, patterns unique to each individual.

The deeper areas of the dermis are filled with a network of tough collagenous and stretchable fibres, which decrease with age and contribute to wrinkle formation. The dermis also contains muscle fibres, hair follicles, sweat and sebaceous glands and many blood vessels (remember the square inch). Nerve endings or receptors make it possible for the skin to act as an enormous sense organ, responding to light touch and pressure and keeping it informed of changes in its environment.

The skin is our first line of defence, protecting against microbial infection, ultraviolet rays from the Sun, harmful chemicals, cuts and tears. It is waterproof and so protects against excessive fluid loss.

Also responsible for temperature regulation, the skin can release about 3000 calories of body heat a day, which would boil 20 litres of water!

It regulates via sweat secretion and bringing blood flow to the body surface, where the excess heat 'radiates' out.

There are three causes of skin problems:

1. *Internal cause*: due to an imbalance of one or more body systems; digestive, nervous, hormonal, etc.; internal bacterial, fungal or viral infections, including acne, eczema, psoriasis, dandruff, rashes, ringworm, dry skin, shingles, warts.
2. *Internal reaction to external causes*: bacterial or chemical including contact dermatitis (e.g. an allergy to nickel). Infected sores and cuts. Blisters. Poison oak or ivy.
3. *External causes*: Cuts, bruises, burns.

When treating the skin, it is important to treat from the inside, as well as from the outside. Support other organs of elimination (lungs, digestive, urinary and lymphatic) with tonic herbs. Also look for hormonal imbalances or stresses and include bitters in your formula.

ACTIONS TO CONSIDER FOR THE SKIN

Alteratives: to move and clear blockages, to cleanse and energise the blood. Chickweed, cleavers, dock, burdock, calendula, dandelion, milk thistle, nettles, plantain, prunella, red clover, sweet violet, yarrow, etc.

Demulcents: moisturise the body from within and nourish the mucous membranes along the digestive, respiratory and urinary systems and will help to correct dry conditions.

Emollients: moisturise the skin from the outside and strengthen the integrity and flexibility of the skin. Demulcent herbs are often emollient and vice versa. Comfrey, chickweed, elder flowers, honey, mallow, marshmallow, oats, rose, chickweed, plantain, etc.

Hepatics/bitters: aid the liver in its detoxification tasks and contribute to hormonal balance. Dandelion root, dock, burdock, vervain, yarrow, elecampane, etc.

Diaphoretics: encourage the pores to open, stimulate the sebaceous glands and bring blood to the surface of the skin to encourage elimination. Catnip, elder, linden, yarrow, apple cider vinegar.

Lymphatics: aid the 'master filter' to do its work. Cleavers, calendula, red clover, apple cider vinegar, deep breathing, laughter (really!), exercise, dry brushing, massage.

Anti-microbials: for bacterial causes, cuts and wounds, to clear and prevent infection and deodorise. Thyme, calendula, sage, yarrow, lavender.

Anti-fungals: for fungal rashes, e.g. athlete's foot, ringworm, dandruff. Calendula, garlic, thyme.

Anti-inflammatories: chickweed, chamomile, liquorice, elder, lavender, honey, oats.

Anti-virals: warts are caused by a virus – to clear warts, clear the virus from the inside. Calendula, lemon balm, St. John's wort, thyme, etc.

Anti-pruritics: alleviate itching. Chickweed, chamomile, lavender, marshmallow, oats, witch hazel.

Astringents: strengthen and tone the skin tissue: for 'weeping' conditions. Geranium, rose, sage, yarrow, witch hazel, etc.

Nutrients: the key to good skin. Chickweed, dandelion, nettles, green leafies.

Vulneraries: for healing bruises, cuts, abrasions, wounds. Calendula, comfrey (not for deep cuts/wounds), prunella, St. John's wort, vervain, yarrow.

ADDITIONAL CONSIDERATIONS

Environment: check for and remove possible irritants. Fabrics (natural only – no polyester). Soaps/detergents – no perfumes or dyes. Cosmetics – it is best to not put anything on your skin that you wouldn't put in your mouth. Ensure enough fresh air, sunlight and water.

Eliminative functions: correct constipation, encourage urination, aid digestion, liver, encourage sweating/exercise, check clothing (can the skin breathe?).

Diet: balanced nutrition, balanced fats (necessary for the absorption of certain vitamins, too much can clog), check for possible allergens. Water, water, water!

Relaxation.

Rest.

Sleep.

Immune system: see all of the above.

TREATING CONDITIONS CAUSED BY INTERNAL FACTORS

Eczema

A non-contagious inflammation, resulting in a sore, itchy, often dry, sometimes-weepy rash. Can be stubborn – patience is required! (Stubbornness and lack of patience may be metaphysical contributors.) *Many causes*: nutritional deficiencies, poor digestion, assimilation, stress, food allergies, dust mites, animal dander, and poor circulation which causes hardening of the arteries.

Herbal formulation

You'll want to base your formula on alteratives, nutrients, nervines and anti-inflammatories.

A possible formula

Nettles – alterative, nutrient.
Chamomile – digestive tonic, nervine, anti-inflammatory (will also help soften stubbornness and enhance patience).
Chickweed – anti-pruretic, alterative, urinary tonic, demulcent, nutrient.
Borage – demulcent, adaptogen, adrenal tonic, will 'soften' stress reactions.

Dietary considerations

Introduce cold-pressed oils – evening primrose, olive, safflower, sunflower.
Carrot juice – provides Vitamin A.

Introduce sources of Vitamin B6 (e.g. comfrey).
Spring tonic or honegar – provides micro-nutrients.
Reduce/eliminate fried foods, alcohol, junk food, sugar.

External

Oatmeal soap/wash.
Sea salt baths.
Poultices/compresses/washes with comfrey, chickweed, plantain, elder,
chamomile.

Psoriasis

A dry, itchy, scaly rash, on the limbs and scalp, affecting about 4% of
people with fair skin. Occurring in cycles of remission and recurrence,
aggravated by stress and tension, the skin keratinocytes over-produce
and fail to mature into normal keratin. The outer layer of skin sloughs
off too quickly, revealing the vulnerable, raw deeper layer. The under-
skin is pink to red, the scales are silvery. Individuals with this syndrome
are often strong constitutionally, yet are tense and isolated, fearful of
being hurt and resistant to getting close to other people. It often runs
in families due to taking on emotional patterns.

While the root cause is unknown, the pattern seems to reflect an auto-
immune condition, sometimes occurring after a bad shock, resulting in
adreno-cortical hormone disturbance. Therefore, do not give immune
tonics as the system is over-stimulated already. Nourish and rest the
immune system instead, giving some attention to the adrenal glands.
Due to stress, the adrenals have been secreting high amounts of adrenalin
and cortico-steroid hormones, putting stress on all the body's systems.
Attend to whole body/mind/spirit nourishment and balance.

Poor Vitamin D synthesis is another factor. Vitamin D is fat-soluble.
Check to see if there is enough oil in the diet and that the individual
is getting enough sunlight. Since we create Vitamin D from sunlight,
psoriasis tends to be more active in winter.

ACTIONS NEEDED

A key herb here is red clover, which normalises skin growths.

Tonics

Skin: calendula, comfrey, elder, *Rosa* spp., nettles (think bioflavanoids),
bitters.

Lymphatic: calendula, chickweed, cleavers, apple cider vinegar.
Urinary: chickweed, cleavers, nettles, red clover.
Nervous: St. John's wort, oatstraw or oats, vervain, violet.
Digestive/hepatics: burdock, chamomile, dandelion, dock, 'spaghetti herbs'.
Adrenal: borage, liquorice.

Alteratives

Burdock, calendula, dock, nettles, dandelion, red clover, sweet violet.

Anti-inflammatories

Chickweed, cleavers, chamomile, comfrey, oats.

Demulcents

Chickweed, comfrey, elder flowers, mallow, marshmallow.

Possible formula

Red clover – alterative, lymphatic, urinary tonic, normalises growth.
Chickweed – alterative, demulcent, anti-pruritic, nutrient, lymphatic and urinary tonic, releases old patterns.
Chamomile – nervous and digestive tonic, calming, anti-inflammatory.
Borage – adrenal tonic, diuretic, demulcent.
Calendula – skin and lymphatic tonic, vulnerary.
Dandelion – bitter, alterative, nutritive.
Administer as tincture – can be alcohol or apple cider vinegar, 3 tsp. per day

Additional therapies

Incorporate at least three cups a day of nutrient teas such as nettles.
Incorporate flower essences and aromatherapy to help shift the emotional patterns.
Topical applications – calendula, comfrey and St. John's wort infused in olive oil with essential oil of lavender. Oatmeal baths.
Incorporate exercise to aid digestion, circulation and elimination.

Fungal rashes

These include ringworm, dandruff, athlete's foot and jock itch. Be sure to include an anti-fungal herb such as calendula in your formulation. Fungus grows in cool, damp conditions, so think warm and sunny!

INTERNAL REACTIONS TO EXTERNAL CAUSES

Contact dermatitis

Remove irritant – jewellery, clothing, perfume, etc.

Create the herbal formulas around anti-histamines to reduce allergic reaction, alteratives, and anti-inflammatories.

Avoid circulatory stimulants, hot, spicy, high-acid foods.

Boils

These are an infection-based skin eruption, triggered by a lowered immune response. They are often an anti-biotic side-effect. Include anti-microbials, immune tonics, alteratives in your formula.

Topical – bentonite clay with a sage essential oil poultice or fresh plantain poultice. Apply and leave for 30 minutes.

Poison oak/poison ivy

Build your formula around alteratives, anti-inflammatories and supporting elimination.

Topical – do not use oils! Poison oak and poison ivy are oils and will only be spread by the use of them.

Apply cooling washes with a spray bottle such as mugwort and peppermint, apple cider vinegar with lavender essential oil. Do not use cloth compresses as this can also facilitate spreading.

Do be sure to wash all clothing, bedding daily and wipe down shoes, tools and anything else that may have been contaminated with rubbing alcohol. These irritant oils can live up to three years!

Take oatmeal baths to soothe and relieve itching.

EXTERNAL CAUSES

First- and second-degree burns

First-degree burns such as sunburn and scalds involve the surface layers of the epidermis, resulting in reddening and minor discomfort. There may be peeling, but no blistering.

Second-degree burns involve the deep epidermal layers and always cause injury to the upper layers of the dermis, including sweat glands, hair follicles and sebaceous glands. Blisters, severe pain, generalised swelling and fluid loss occur.

Lavender is the herb for burns, hands down! In its essential oil form, make sure that it is *Lavendula off.* or *L. augustofolia*. It is the most effective first-aid remedy. I once poured a pot of boiling water over my hand and by rights, I should have had a second-to-third-degree burn. I put lavender essential oil directly on my hand and, other than a little redness, it healed quickly and perfectly, with no pain, blistering or scarring! Another time, while leading a vision quest, I put my hand on a metal candle-lantern, burning it badly, only this time, the lavender oil someone had was not the *L. off.* or *L. augustofolia* species and it didn't do anything! It was a painful way to learn that lesson!

Additional herbs to consider post-emergency

St. John's wort – anti-inflammatory, repairs nerve damage.
Comfrey – demulcent, emollient, repairs tissue damage.
Calendula – repairs tissue damage, prevents scarring.
Nutrients.
Demulcents.
Emollients.
Nervine tonics.

A possible formula

> St. John's wort – 2 parts
> Comfrey – 1 part
> Calendula – 1 part
> Nettles – 2 parts
> Chickweed – 2 parts

Application

1 tsp. 3 times a day, continuing for two weeks after the burn 'looks' healed.

Topical

20 drops lavender essential oil in 1 cup of cool calendula and comfrey tea. Pour into a spray bottle and spray the burn area many times a day. Dress with light non-stick bandage or 'bentonite second skin', made as follows.

Make a wet paste with 1 part bentonite clay and at least 2 parts water. Make sure the clay particles are completely absorbed into the water. Add 10 drops lavender for every cup of clay. Apply a 1-inch layer to the burn and cover with something that will keep the clay wet: plastic wrap, wet gauze, or comfrey leaves, for example. Watch carefully that the pack doesn't dry out. You want the fluid to be reabsorbed back into the skin from the blister, not out of the blister into the clay! Change every 4 hours for up to 3 days.

RECIPES FOR THE SKIN

Aside from all the emergencies and imbalances, taking good care of our skin is vital to good health. Since ancient times, we have used 'cosmetics', not simply for vanity, but to nourish and honour our whole body. The ancients observed daily rituals of bathing and anointing. By making our own bodycare products, we can take our consumer dollars away from the corporations that own the companies that make commercial cosmetics, often using animal testing to prove their results. Not to mention, home-made herbal bodycare is a wonderfully sensual experience and contributes greatly to our sense of well-being! The following recipes are akin to those used in very expensive retail products.

Earth mud #1 – a moisturising face scrub

> 1 cup cornflour.
> 1 cup oatflour.
> $\frac{1}{2}$ cup bentonite clay.
> $1\frac{1}{2}$ cups honey.
> $\frac{1}{2}$ cup Queen of Hungary water.
> $\frac{1}{2}$ cup marshmallow tea.
> 10 drops carrot seed essential oil.
> 10 drops rose geranium essential oil.
> 5 drops lemon oil.

Mix dry ingredients together. Mix in honey, then Queen of Hungary water, then marshmallow tea. Spoon into a wide-mouthed jar and keep on the bathroom sink to cleanse face.

Earth mud #2 – a body scrub

> One cup each of cornflour, oatflour, bentonite clay.
> 2 cups honey.
> Enough comfrey tea to make a thick paste.
> Your favourite combination of essential oils, about 25 drops total.

Mix together and spoon into a wide-mouth jar. Keep by the bath. Take a scoop into your hands and scrub away!

Queen of Hungary's water

This is the skin potion reputed to have been brought to the dying Queen of Hungary, renowned for her beauty, back to life when it was administered to her by a handsome stranger! No one was ever able to determine whether it was the handsome stranger or the potion that healed her, but since we don't always have access to a handsome stranger, at least we have the potion! There are actually several variations on this traditional recipe, the following is the one I make.

When the Moon is in Taurus or Libra (ruled by Venus), make a combination apple cider vinegar tincture from equal parts:

> Rose petals
> Lemon balm
> Rosemary
> Lavender
> Sage
> Orange peel

Allow to infuse for a Moon cycle, strain and then dilute 1 part Queen's water with 5 parts pure water. Add 5 drops lavender essential oil to each ounce of dilution. Use as a makeup remover, toner/astringent, hair rinse, bath or even salad dressing! (Remember? Don't put anything on your skin.)

CREAMS AND LOTIONS

To make a cream

Basic ingredients

> $\frac{1}{2}$ cup oil.
> $\frac{1}{2}$ cup water.
> $\frac{1}{4}$ cup shaved beeswax.
> 10 drops essential oils.

Tools

> A good-sized copper bowl.
> A fine whisk.
> 2 pots – one which you'll want to keep only for oils.

Now consider how you want to embellish the oil and water to add enhancing ingredients to the formula. For example, use comfrey infused oil and rose petal tea, or you might choose plain almond oil and a comfrey, elder blossom and calendula flower tea. Decide what essential oils you'd like to use both for aroma and therapy. Consider vulnerary, emollient, and anti-inflammatory properties.

Assemble your ingredients and tools.

Start your tea and, over a low heat, melt your beeswax into your oil. Let the tea and the oil cool to room temperature. Put the tea and essential oils into the copper bowl, and place it under your 'passive' arm. With your 'active' hand, pour the oil into the tea, grab your whisk and beat (like mad!) in a spiralling motion. When the cream has 'homogenised', place the cream immediately in sterile jars. Store in a cool place.

You may also make this cream in a blender, although I like the old-fashioned method myself. Put your 'water part' and essential oils in the blender. Put the lid on without the centre bit. Turn the blender on to medium-high speed and slowly drizzle in your 'oil part'. This is the same procedure as making mayonnaise and may take a little practice at first!

You may end up with a 'grainy' cream – this means that the oil/beeswax or the water part was too cold.

Because these creams are made of all natural ingredients, they are fragile and have a short shelf life, so make small amounts and use them generously!

Celtic mist

An oil-free, renewing, moisturising spray/lotion for the face and body. It is beneficial for dry skin as a makeup remover and toner and for oily skin as a light moisturiser.

> 1 oz. dilute Queen of Hungary's water.
> 4 oz. red rose petal tea (red will give the colour).
> 2 oz. vegetable glycerine.
> $\frac{1}{2}$ oz. Vitamin E oil.
> 2 drops rose essential oil or 10 drops rose geranium oil.

Shake well before use. Apply liberally with a cotton pad or from a spray bottle. (I like to use clear bottles in this case, because the liquids resolve into beautiful layers of colour when not shaken.)

WEAVING THE WEB

Suggestions for working with the Element of Earth and the lessons of this chapter.

Make an altar to honour the Earth. Contemplate your own relationship with the Earth (I'm sure many of you have been doing this for some time).

Make an incense of Earth and set it to the East on your altar.

Make an oil of Earth and anoint an Earth coloured candle. Set it in the South.

Choose an 'earthy' vessel to hold the water blessing. Set it in the West.

Set a bowl of grain, berries, seeds, stones, etc. and place it in the North.

You have just made a ritual of nurturing for our Mother Earth – believe that your blessing makes a difference!

Gather the three herbs of the Materia Medica *and work with them in various ways. Record your experiences. Pay attention to how they affect your physical senses.*

Study the section on the skin. Make a skin tonic tea and the cosmetic recipes and use them for two weeks. Notice any difference?

Make a house blessing ritual for your own home, cleaning it first with some of the natural recipes. You might want to do this prior to setting up your Earth altar. Take note of the energy of the house before and after.

Blessings of Brighid on your house!

CHAPTER 6

CELTIC DEITIES OF HEALING

THE TUATHA DE DANNAN

Airmid

Irish patroness of herbalists, keeper of the sacred knowledge of healing with plants. Invoke Airmid's blessings when you're in the medicine garden, making your herbal products and creating formulas. Airmid helps us to choose the right ones.

Brighid

The consummate deity of healing, for all physical, mental, emotional and spiritual issues. Refer to previous notes!

The Cailleach

'The Old Wise One', she is there to help us with issues concerning our past, loss, sorrow, death. There in the deep darkness, she will ladle out a cup of tea from her cauldron and, in her great wisdom, will help us come to terms, heal and be reborn into a new beginning. The Cailleach is found in caves, forests, craggy hilltops and, whenever we are lonely, grieving or lost. She is the midwife of death and rebirth.

Herbs to honour the Cailleach – elderberries, sage, dried hawthorn berries, poppy.

Dagda

'The Good Father', Dagda aids healing in issues concerning relationship with men, particularly fathers. A wonderful role model for men, perceived as extremely strong and stout, with arms and legs like tree trunks, Dagda has a great sense of humour and an equally great love for the common folk. He presides over the Cauldron of Plenty and offers us nourishment for our bodies and our spirits. All you have to do is ask and he will serve you up your favourite food. He is a god of prosperity and abundant harvest and he calls in the changing seasons with the music of his harp.

Herbs to honour the Dagda – oak, oats.

The Morrigan

'Great Queen', Triple Goddess, Dark Goddess. The Morrigan was raped by an enemy and gave birth to a monster with three hearts. She had to make the terrible decision to put the being to death or it would have destroyed the world. Her keening ripped through her vocal cords so that, forever after, her voice was like the ravens, who are her birds. She retreated to the Underworld and became its Queen. It is to her dark, soft womb we go when we die, there to rest and prepare for rebirth. She is night and depth and mystery. She is a Triple Goddess, Warrior-Maiden, Queen and Crone. Ask the Morrigan's aid in healing all forms of abuse, identifying your Shadow self, banishing dis-ease and vandals and releasing negative patterns. Like us, she has experienced violence and has survived, she has known loss and grief and has survived. She will understand.

Herbs to honour the Morrigan – nettles, sage, poppies, dark red roses, elderberries.

Aongus MacOg

'Aongus the Youthful', Celtic God of Love. Lonely? Failing in the romance department? Suffering a broken heart? Aongus can help!

Aongus is the 'love-child' of Boann and the Dagda, born at Bru na Boinne/Newgrange. When he speaks, his words become birds, flying out into the world to spread his blessings. Aongus is the protector of lovers and the unloved. He will visit lonely women in their dreams and comfort them, until self-esteem is restored and a new lover comes along. He is a role model for all lovers as he supports Caer, his own beloved, in being fully herself. (She likes to live as a swan half the year. He decides he will too, then, so that he can be with her.) Aongus can help to heal a broken heart of rejection, bitterness and cynicism. He restores youthfulness and innocence.

Herbs to honour Aongus – wild oats, primroses, wild roses.

RITUAL FOR HEALING

Let the individual who is to receive the healing meditate on releasing the disease and receiving the blessings. They could recite 'The Prayer of the Chalice' from Chapter 4.

Prepare beforehand the blessings of the four Airts.

Air

Incense

A possible recipe

1 part vervain – to invoke the healing spirit, honour the sacred.
1 part thyme – strengthens the immune system, invokes the aid of the Deity.
1 part rosemary – to speed the healing.
1 part lady's mantle – invokes Brighid's aid around the healing.

Fire

Candles of the appropriate, meaningful colour. White or natural beeswax if you can't decide.

A healing oil

Infuse in olive oil,
  1 part vervain.
  1 part willow.
  1 part wormwood.

Infuse herbs in the oil for a full Moon cycle. Strain, bottle and use for anointing.

Water

A beautiful cup with pure spring water or a healing tea or a flower essence.

Earth

Herbs, a crystal or stone that represents the individual being healed.

Create an altar with the four blessings. Have the individual lie or sit in a comfortable position. Invoke the deity/s of healing. Work around the four Airs, beginning with the blessing of Air. Say a prayer, asking each element's blessing on the individual.

Example

> *Blessed Brighid, Lady of Air, blow away this illness with the next wind.*
>
> *Blessed Brighid, Lady of Fire, gently burn away this disease with the next rising of the Sun.*
>
> *Blessed Brighid, Lady of the healing waters, wash away this disease with the next wave of the sea.*
>
> *Blessed Brighid, Lady of Earth, make this body whole again.*

Be creative and relevant to the individual receiving the healing.

End by thanking the Elements and the Deity invoked.

Let the individual rest and meditate on the healing energies.

Follow up with appropriate herbal and other holistic therapies.

Clear the air of the sickness that has been released by burning lavender and thyme or spraying with lavender and thyme essential oil and water.

THE ENDOCRINE SYSTEM

Communication and control of the whole body occur through the nervous and endocrine systems. The nervous system communicates via electrical impulses and the endocrine system communicates via chemical secretion.

Hormones are complex chemicals produced by patches of cells called glands.

They are classified by their molecular structure as polypeptides, steroids and amines.

Polypeptides and amines are made from amino acids and steroids are made from cholesterol.

Hormones are the chemical messengers, communicating and triggering responses throughout the body. Like all chemical constituents in the body, they are derived from food materials – protein, fats and carbohydrates.

The glands create the chemicals or hormones, then secrete them into tissue or the bloodstream, or else into a drainage duct.

If the chemical is secreted via a duct, the gland is called an exocrine gland. Sweat glands are exocrine glands. If the hormone is secreted directly into the blood or tissue, it is an endocrine gland.

Because hormones are very powerful chemicals, only minute amounts are produced as required. As they are carried all around the body, in the bloodstream, they pass through numerous organs. However, they are specialised to cause an effect in only very specific parts of the body.

The hormones are secreted into intercellular spaces, then diffused directly into the blood and carried throughout the body. Each hormone molecule may then bind to a cell, called a target organ cell, that has specific receptors for that hormone. Think of the hormone as the key and the target organ cell or receptor site as the lock.

Hormones are the main regulators of metabolism, growth and development, reproduction and homeostasis, including fluid, electrolyte, acid and energy balances.

Vibrant health is a direct result of an efficiently communicating endocrine system!

A whole and fully connected lifestyle, including good nutrition, exercise, a positive emotional and spiritual life, nourishes and balances the endocrine glands.

The whole body can be healed through the endocrine system!

Bitter herbs will stimulate hormonal secretion!

THE SPECIFIC GLANDS

Knowledge of the endocrine system is much more ancient than the current allopathic 'understanding' of it. Just look at the Eastern Indian system of the Chakras. To the Celtic Druids, the chakras were known as 'light centres'. Each centre is perceived as a 'gateway' to particular energies, as connections to The Source. If the centres are clogged, suppressed, un-nourished, then imbalance and, ultimately, illness occurs. No matter how much the endocrine system is studied in Western allopathic medicine, much of it still remains a mystery! The Ancients understood that these light centres are the gateways to the mysteries and the mystery is infinite! They are unique to each unique individual and the mysteries are to be approached again and again, each time revealing new layers of understanding. The endocrine system also illustrates so beautifully the necessity for *holistic* treatment. There is no one pill or herb – treatment must encompass the *whole* lifestyle or true healing can't occur. I have seen profound healing occur when the attitude of the client transforms from a negative one to a positive one.

THE PITUITARY GLAND

Located at the base of the brain, the pituitary is the Master Gland, controlling all the other glands and acting as mediator between the chemical endocrine messages and the electrical nervous system messages. As Guardian of Cycles, it receives communication from all other parts of the body, via the hypothalamus gland. It is located on the undersurface of the brain, above and behind the nasal cavity. It is affected by light and there are two lobes, the anterior and the posterior.

The anterior lobe secretes at least six different hormones:

1. Melanophore is a stimulating hormone which acts on pigment cells of the skin.
2. Prolactin controls milk secretion.
3. Somatotropin or growth hormone stimulates development of bone and other tissue, and influences sugar regulation by the pancreas.
4. Two gonadotrophic hormones (FSH and LH) stimulate activity in the testes or ovaries.
5. Thyrotrophic hormone (TSH) stimulates thyroid secretions.
6. Adrenocorticotrophic stimulates adrenal secretion of the hormone, cortisol.

The posterior lobe stores and secrete

1. Oxytocin stimulates uterine contractions and milk production.
2. Antidiuretic hormone (ADH) tells the kidneys to reduce urine production

Actual production of these two hormones occurs in the hypothalamus.

THE HYPOTHALAMUS

The hypothalamus gland is the connecting link between the endocrine and nervous systems and is located next to the pituitary. Responsible for many body functions, the hypothalamus regulates hunger, thirst, sleep, wakefulness, body temperature, sexual drive and the menstrual cycle by secreting releasing and inhibiting hormones to the pituitary gland, in addition to secreting ADH and oxytocin.

THE PINEAL GLAND

The pineal gland is a small, pine-cone-shaped gland located in the centre of the brain. It regulates the onset of puberty and the menstrual cycle. It stops gonadotrophic hormone release with a deficiency resulting in too early puberty or sex gland problems.

The pineal gland is directly affected by light and, responding to sensory input from the optic nerves, it acts as our internal clock, secreting melatonin on a 24 hour cycle, with blood levels being highest at night, causing drowsiness.

The pineal gland directly corresponds to the Third Eye.

TONICS TO STRENGTHEN THE PITUITARY, HYPOTHALAMUS AND PINEAL GLANDS

Colour therapy: Violet and deep blue. Visualise, wear and decorate with these colours.
Herbs: Bitters, rosemary, gingko, violet, peppermint.
Light therapy: Get at least 10 minutes of natural sunlight a day. Try to sleep under natural moonlight. No nightlights, please!
Meditation.
Music therapy.

THE THYROID GLAND

The thyroid secretes:

1. Thyroxin (T4) – contains iodine with an amino acid, which increases metabolic rate.
2. Triiodothyronine (T3).

The two together make up thyroid hormone.
Hypothyroid (low thyroid secretions) = slow metabolism.
Hyperthyroid (high thyroid secretions) = fast metabolism.

Calcitonin lowers the concentration of calcium in the blood, counteracting the effect of parathormone, produced by the parathyroid.

THE PARATHYROID GLAND

The parathyroid gland secretes parathormone, which helps regulate the balance of calcium in the blood and adjusts the rate at which it is excreted through the urine.

Thyroid imbalances

Hyperthyroidism increased secretions of thyroxin 'turn up' metabolism, resulting in a greater need for oxygen. Often manifests in menopausal women. Symptoms include:

Feeling hot when the environment is cool.
Palpitations.
Irritability.
Hyperactivity.
Poor sleep.
Weight loss.
Protruding eyes.

Hypothyroidism – thyroid deficiency

In babies, it manifests as underdevelopment, mentally and physically. It develops into cretinism; short in stature, thick, coarse skin and hair, a fat, protruding tongue and rounded belly. Early treatment with thyroxin hormone can be completely successful.

Myxoedema manifests in adults, most often menopausal women. Symptoms include:

Fatigue not helped by sleep.
Feeling cold.
Heart palpitations.
Constipation, sluggish digestion.
Increase in weight.
Sore, hoarse throat.
Dry, coarse skin.
Poor concentration, intellectual acuity.
Hair falls out from outer third of eyebrows.
Numbness in hands and feet.
Lethargy, depression, crying, emotional.
Dark circles and swelling under eyes.

Therapies for hyperthyroidism and hypothyroidism

When we are working with a gland or a system that is too low or too high, we work to bring balance, therefore the treatment is the same. See above.

Nervine tonics and bitters.
Mineral rich herbs like nettles and dandelion.
Dandelion is *the* tonic herb for the thyroid – whole plant, please.
Circulatory tonics – rosemary, yarrow, etc.
Alteratives – dock, yarrow, etc.
Myrrh essential oil in a carrier rubbed into throat area helps to balance
    secretions.
Foods – onions, seafood, organics (from iodine-rich soil).
Kelp and other seaweeds, cabbage, cress, spinach.
Sea salt as condiment and in bath.
Hydrotherapy – fluctuating hot and cold.
Breath therapy.
Communication therapy – singing helps too!
Colour therapy – blue.

THE THYMUS GLAND

The thymus gland plays a key role in immunity, secreting thymosin, which promotes the development of white blood cells.

The thymus gland is 'the school' where white blood cells learn to recognise antigens. This is called cell-mediated immunity. It is very active during childhood when many antigens are being experienced for the first time.

The herb, thyme, is one of the best for energising and healing an underactive thymus gland. Its high content of essential oil, which contains thymosine, provides immunity while rejuvenating and strengthening the body's natural immunity.

THE PANCREAS

The pancreas plays the key role in blood sugar balance. The islet cells of the pancreas secrete:

1. insulin, which facilitates the passage of glucose from the bloodstream into cells of tissues that require it, lowering blood glucose levels, and

2. glucagon, which triggers the breakdown of glycogen to glucose, raising the blood glucose levels.

Therapies

Remove sugar from the diet – give the body a chance to find its own blood sugar balance. Do NOT use sugar substitutes like aspartame, etc.

Dandelion flowers are a specific tonic for the pancreas. Use whole plant as the leaves and roots will help the kidneys and liver in their role in balancing hormones.

THE ADRENAL GLANDS

The two adrenal glands are about the size of walnuts and one sits on top of each kidney. They are responsible for maintaining the balance of many body functions by secreting several important hormones that affect carbohydrate metabolism. These hormones share similar chemical structure (all steroids) and three different types of function:

1. Cortisol regulates the laying down of body fat. Suppresses inflammation and allergic reactions. (Allergy-prone people need adrenal tonics!)
2. Aldosterone prevents excess loss of salt and water in the form of urine. Regulates the balance between sodium and potassium.
3. Secretes the sex hormones of both males and females.

The adrenal medulla, the inner portion of the gland, secretes adrenaline and noradrenalin, directly affecting the sympathetic nervous system. The adrenal medulla maintains nervous control over involuntary body functions such as heart rate, respiration, digestion, etc.

The adrenal cortex, the outer portion, secretes corticosteroids, which are formed from cholesterol. These include mineral corticoids, glucocorticoids and keto-steroids.

Taking care of our adrenals is important during and after stressful times and particularly important for menopausal women as the adrenals take over the function for our ovaries when they 'retire'.

Therapies

Borage is the tonic herb for the adrenal glands. It can be administered without fear of side effects.

Combine with kidney tonics such as dandelion. Incorporate nervine tonics such as oatstraw or violet. High mineral herbs and foods. Rest! Avoid stimulants of any kind. Drink lots of water.

THE GONADS

The ovaries secrete oestrogen, which stimulates ovulation and libido; and progesterone, which triggers menstruation

The testicles secrete testosterone, which affects male sex organs and contributes to male characteristics.

See chapters on specific reproductive systems for in-depth therapies.

Study, contemplate, and meditate on the following correspondences. Can you make any connections between emotional issues and physical balances you may have experienced?

HERBAL CARE FOR BABIES AND CHILDREN

Newborn to 2 years

3 drops of tincture diluted in $\frac{1}{4}$ cup water, expressed breast milk, formula or juice.

$\frac{1}{8}$ cup of tea, 3 times a day – can be mixed with juice to increase palatability.

Nursing mothers can take the adult dose and the herb will pass through the breast milk to the child.

Do NOT give honey to infants under 1 year old.

2 to 6 years

$\frac{1}{4}$ cup of tea, three times a day.
6 to 10 drops of tincture in $\frac{1}{4}$ cup of water, three times a day.

6 to 12 years

$\frac{1}{2}$ cup of tea, three times a day.
10–20 drops of tincture in $\frac{1}{4}$ cup of water, three times a day.

12 to adult

1 cup of tea, three times a day.
20–40 drops of tincture in $\frac{1}{4}$ cup of water.

BABY CARE

Eye care

2 tsp. fennel or chamomile infused in 4 oz. of boiling water and strained through non-bleached coffee filters twice. Store in the refrigerator in a sterile jar and apply with eyedropper or cotton pad three times a day.

Jaundice

This occurs pretty commonly in newborns and easily remedied with exposure to gentle sunlight.

Breast feeding

Dandelion or catnip tea (drunk by the mother and passed through breast-milk).

Diaper rash

Expose baby's bottom to air and gentle sunlight. Change diapers often – use a mild soap and add apple cider vinegar to rinse cycle. Use calendula and lavender tea as a wash at diapering.

Please do not use talc powders – the talc is tiny sharp slivers that irritate sensitive skin.

Softly healing baby powder

2 parts arrowroot powder.
$\frac{1}{4}$ part powdered comfrey leaf.
$\frac{1}{4}$ part powdered calendula petals.

Diaper rash ointment

$\frac{1}{3}$ cup comfrey oil.
$\frac{1}{3}$ cup calendula oil.
$\frac{1}{3}$ cup St. John's wort oil.
$\frac{1}{4}$ cup beeswax.
15–20 drops lavender essential oil.

Make as a salve and apply at each diapering.

Uncircumcised penis infection

Follow same steps as with diaper rash with the exception of the salve. Instead, mix 10 drops of myrrh essential oil in 1 cup of water – apply with cotton pad at each diaper change. If you can't obtain myrrh, use lavender, sage or 5 drops of thyme. You can also make strong cups of lavender, sage or thyme tea and apply in the same way.

Teething pain

Symptoms – low fever, diaper rash, congestion, irritability

Preventive measures – calcium intake is very important. Mother should drink lots of raspberry, blackberry and/or nettle tea and pass through the breast milk or offer light infusions in a bottle.

Do NOT use clove oil – this is an adult remedy and can burn baby's tender gums. Instead, apply drops of strong tepid chamomile tea directly to the area with a dropper. Also offer chamomile tea ice chips.

Catnip tea and rescue remedy will help mother and child with frayed nerves and fever.

Thrush (*Candida albicans*)

A fungal rash. Symptoms – redder mouth with white patches, flaky, inflamed skin in baby's throat and mouth, mother's nipples, folds of arms and genitals.

Practise careful hygiene – mother should wash nipples and swab baby's mouth with calendula tea after every breastfeeding.

Apply organic yoghurt in mouth and on skin patches.

Soak plantain seeds overnight and apply gel to skin patches.

Mother should reduce/eliminate sugar and dairy from diet temporarily.

Colic

An extreme amount of air in the digestive tract. Causes are insufficient digestive enzymes, hypersensitive nervous system and/or nervous tension in mother/father/baby/environment.

Symptoms – Baby screams while drawing legs up to the chest. Baby's mouth stays wide and rigidly open. Baby is in a lot of pain!

Emergency measures

Lay the baby, tummy side down, along the length of your arm. Pat and rub back gently. This will help disperse the gas.

As soon as the baby will take it, give a bottle of fennel or chamomile tea.

Preventive measures

De-stress the home! Attend to the creation of peaceful, harmonious surroundings.

Try changes in colour, sound (e.g. music), air quality.

Adults in the household need to work on peaceful emotions.

Breastfed babies

Mother should avoid foods in the cabbage family – broccoli, brussels sprouts, turnips, radishes, kale, collards, cauliflower, onions, garlic.

Also avoid chocolate, peanut butter, sugar and white flour.

Drink nervine teas before breastfeeding – chamomile, catnip, fennel.

Bottlefed babies

Avoid all of the above. Try goat's milk formula.

Give a light infusion of chamomile, catnip or fennel tea $-\frac{1}{8}$ cup to 8 oz. before formula bottle.

Give acidophalus culture (yoghurt, kefir) to build up beneficial digestive flora, $\frac{1}{4}$ tsp. 4–5 times a day.

Apply warm packs over baby's tummy to help relax spasms.

Cradle cap

Cause – overactive sweat or oil glands on scalp create a yellowish, scaly crust on scalp.

Apply olive oil to scalp at night and remove oil and crust with a warm washcloth in the morning.

Several times a day, apply a cool witch hazel infusion to the scalp.

Fevers

Nursing mothers can treat through the breastmilk, drinking a tea of catnip, fennel and elder 3–5 times a day.

Bottlefed babies can be given a 10 minute infusion of the same tea 3–5 times a day.

Both can be given sponge baths of elder and lavender tea 3 times a day.

Keep baby warm and give lots of love and attention.

SPECIAL BABYCARE PRODUCTS

Baby lotion

$\frac{3}{4}$ cup almond oil.
$\frac{3}{4}$ cup calendula and rose petal tea.
$\frac{1}{4}$ cup beeswax.

Warm almond oil and beeswax together. When cooled to skin temperature, add to tea in a copper bowl and whisk until emulsified. Add 10 drops of lavender or chamomile essential oil. Store in a sterile jar.

Baby bath oil

Infuse a light fixed oil with any combination of calendula, chamomile, lavender or rose petals. Strain and add 10 drops of lavender, chamomile or rose essential oils. Store in a sterile bottle and use 1 tablespoon in baby's bath.

Baby sleep pillow

Rose petals
Lavender flowers
Chamomile flowers
Catnip leaves

Mix equal parts and stuff a small muslin pillow form. Stitch closed. Adults like these too!

Herbs for children – over 18 months

Herbs can be administered to children as teas, tinctures, glycerites and baths. Generally use lighter infusions and always drop tincture into boiling water to dissipate the alcohol.

Nourishing herbs

Rich in vitamins and minerals. Nettles, raspberry/blackberry leaf, oatstraw, chickweed, rosehips.

Any of the nourishing herbs can be combined and taken as tea, up to 3 cups a day. The tea can be mixed juice for flavour or a little honey can be added.

Herbs for respiratory infections

Sinus infections

Thyme – fights infection – tea or tincture.
Lemon balm – anti-viral, calming nervine – tincture.
Elder flowers – anti-catarrhal – tea or tincture.
Hyssop – clears congestion, runny nose – tea or tincture.
Rose hips – provides Vitamin C, mildly astringent – tea or tincture.

Clear nose tea

Decoct rosehips. Add equal parts of thyme, elder and hyssop. Add 1 tsp. lemon balm tincture, cover and allow to steep for 10 minutes.

Let the child breathe in the steam from the tea while drinking. Offer $\frac{1}{2}$ cup up to 4 times a day.

Fever

Catnip – increases perspiration without raising internal heat.
Lemon balm – lowers temperature.
Elder/yarrow combined – manage fever.
Thyme – anti-septic, antibacterial.
Lavender – lowers temperature.

Choose the herb appropriate to the stage of fever. Use elder/yarrow to manage normal range fevers (99–101 °F), catnip to stimulate slow moving fevers (it just seems to stay around 100–101 °F and the child doesn't perspire), lemon balm tincture and lavender baths to bring down a spiking fever (102–104 °F). Above that, get them to the hospital. Thyme, combined with any of the above, will deal with the infection that's causing the fever.

Give lots of fluids to drink.

Ear infections

Ear infections are very common in children up to 4 years of age as the ear canals are not completely developed. The ear canals don't drain well, particularly when congested or exposed to cold. Bacteria builds up and infection sets in. Treat at the first signs which include runny nose, head congestion, fuzziness and irritability, rubbing of ears. Ear infections can also be a result of an allergy, possibly to wheat, dairy or citrus.

Always treat both ears even if only one is infected. Make sure ear drums aren't perforated.

Keep the ears warm!

Mullein flowers infused in olive oil – place 1 drop in each ear 3 times a day.

Garlic oil – see above.

Onion poultice – in addition to one of the above. Chop an onion and fry in a little olive oil until soft, but not completely cooked. Allow to cool enough that it won't burn tender skin. Wrap 2 tablespoons in a clean muslin cloth and place over the ear. Leave for 10 minutes. Treat the other ear.

Also give thyme or hyssop tea to aid the immune system from within.

Lung congestion with cough

Coltsfoot – demulcent and anti-inflammatory to mucus membranes.
Mullein leaf – soothes and relaxes lung tissue. Coltsfoot and mullein work
    well together.
Hyssop – anti-inflammatory and soothing nervine.
Fennel – expectorant-clears bronchial passages.
Honey – soothes cough.
Make an 'equal parts' tea of the above with honey added.
Onion poultice on chest.

Soothing cough syrup

Decoct equal parts fennel seeds and rosehips. Add equal parts mullein, coltsfoot and hyssop. Allow to steep for 20 minutes. Strain. Add $\frac{1}{2}$ cup honey to every cup of tea.

Store in a sterile bottle and give a teaspoon as needed for cough.

HERBS FOR DIGESTIVE TROUBLES

Nausea

> Chamomile or peppermint – 1 part
> Meadowsweet – 1 part
> Thyme – $\frac{1}{4}$ part

Mix together dried herbs for tea. Offer by the spoonful as often as they'll take it, up to 3 cups a day.

Diarrhoea

The body's way of expelling the bacteria or other substance that is causing the diarrhoea. Strong astringent herbs are often suggested, but this can 'dry up' the intestines too much so that the bacteria remain in the body. Like fever, diarrhoea is an ally and needs to be managed. Dehydration is the real danger, so give plenty of liquids and baths.

> Chamomile – 1 part
> Raspberry or blackberry or strawberry leaf – 1 part
> Meadowsweet – 1 part
> Thyme – $\frac{1}{4}$ part

Make as tea and offer up to 3 cups a day.

Also give cooked applesauce with cinnamon to soothe and cleanse the intestinal tract.

Constipation

Use demulcent herbs to soothe and strengthen the mucus membranes of the intestinal tract. Offer lots of liquids and fibrous fruits and vegetables. Massage the lower abdomen, beginning on the lower right, working up and across, then down the left side. Exercise.

Dandelion root – encourages digestive secretions
Marshmallow root – very demulcent
Decoct equal parts and give up to 3 cups a day.

HERBS FOR COMMON CHILDHOOD INFECTIONS

Measles (Roseola)

This is a viral infection. Once diagnosed, it can be treated effectively with anti-viral herbs and herbs specific to the symptoms. Quarantine and acute nursing are required. Actions should include the following:

Anti-virals – thyme, lemon balm, yarrow, catnip.
Febrifuge – yarrow, elder, catnip.
Lavender in the bath will lower temperature and alleviate itching..
Lymphatics – calendula, red clover.
Anti-inflammatory – thyme, lemon balm.

A possible recipe

> Thyme – 1 part
> Yarrow – 1 part
> Elder – 1 part
> Calendula – 1 part

Make a strong tea and sweeten with honey.

External symptomatic relief

Itching from rash – add oatmeal, along with lavender, to the bath. Nervine teas – oatstraw, chamomile.

Give lots of liquids, keep the child warm, give lots of sponge baths, quiet music and be prepared to entertain the child when the 48 hour crisis period is over! Continue treatment for two weeks.

WEAVING THE WEB

Suggestions for working with the Celtic Deities of Healing and the lessons of this chapter

Create an altar to honour the Deities and invite them into your life. Burn incense, light candles and offer libations and food. Speak to them as you would dear friends.

Obtain the three herbs of the Materia Medica and work with them. Record your experiences.

Meditate on your light centres. Note which centres seem easy and flowing and which seem 'blocked' in some way. Identify the corresponding emotional issue. Endeavour to nurture and unlock them with colour and herbal therapy. Perhaps use your colours on your healing altar.

Create a ritual of healing for yourself, then for someone else (if you haven't done so already!). Record your experiences.

Is there a child/children in your life? You could create a herbal childcare kit, addressing some of the most common issues. Label your products with very clear instructions for use.

CHAPTER 7

REPRODUCTIVE HEALTH – WOMEN

LUNATHYME

Menstruation – the state of formlessness between manifestations . . .

Menstrual blood is the original blood sacrifice to the Mother. We women had no need to cut ourselves or others in order to offer this sacred life-giving substance. All other 'sacrificial rites' were born from the originating menstrual rituals. In the first days of humanity and for aeons until the advent of patriarchy, women gathered together in a sacred place when they bled. With no electrical interruptions, women tended to bleed at the same time, except for those who were pregnant or menopausal.

The bleeding women were released from their daily responsibilities, which were taken over by the other women and the pre-adolescent girls. The bleeding women retreated to a sacred cave, lodge or temple to pray and give their blood to nourish the Mother. During this 3 or 4 day period, they would receive visions and dreams, which they would take back to the community. The community revered women's Blood Mysteries as absolutely sacred and the menstrual time was considered to be an extremely powerful psychic time.

This is the time when women release built up tension and cleanse their bodies and their psyches.

It is being accepted more and more by the scientific/medical realm that the releasing of our blood actually contributes to our health and longevity. It has been shown that high iron levels in the body leads to the build-up of vascular plaque, increasing the possibility of heart disease (the reason why the statistics for heart attacks in men are higher).

Women release excess iron every month! Hmmm! Could this be one of the reasons why women generally live longer? Could this be why the taking of birth control pills and other synthetic hormone therapies actually mess with Nature's wisdom and lead to the rising numbers of women suffering from heart disease? Common sense tells me Yes!

I believe passionately that it is imperative that women reclaim the sacredness of their blood and that we pass this on to the following generations! I have seen, over and over again, the healing and empowerment that this brings to women's psyches and self-esteem! I have seen the correlation in history between the ceasing of women giving their blood to nourish the Mother (now we flush it down the toilet as just another 'waste') and the escalation of war and violence!

The release of the menstrual blood normally occurs about every 28 days, the same amount of time that it takes the Moon to move through a full cycle. The bleeding time averages about 3–4 days. Every woman is unique, however, and there can be many variations to this cycle without necessarily indicating that anything is 'wrong'.

Menstruation is a time when a woman, ideally, turns within. I call it 'the Dragon going into her cave'. It is a time for being with our self, getting reacquainted with all our aspects, including our Shadow. We are Inanna, descending into the Underworld to meet with our Shadow-sister, Erishkagel; we are the Maiden, Cernal, descending to the centre of the Earth to receive wisdom from the Wise One, Cerridwen. A version of this mythology and ritual appears and is honoured in almost every indigenous culture in the world!

When we can't take the time or give ourselves permission to take this restorative journey, our bodies will create symptoms such as cramps, irritability, and infections until we 'get off the treadmill' and do so. Levels of progesterone are lowest at this time, signalling the sloughing of the endometrial lining.

Follicular phase – the maiden/waxing moon phase

The follicle is developing. We begin to feel more outward, energy increases, and our bodies need more protein and oestrogen levels rise. There is often a feeling of euphoria at this time.

Ovulation – the mother/full moon phase

Occuring approximately 12–14 days after the first day of menstruation, lasting about 3–5 days.

The pituitary begins the secretion process of LH (leutenising hormone) and FSH (follicle stimulating hormone). A time of feeling open, very energetic. Oestrogen levels peak.

Luteal phase – the crone/waning moon phase

We begin to feel more inward, the liver is breaking down old hormones, progesterone and oestrogen levels rise, then fall. This is the time when we are most prone to pre-menstrual tension – Ancient Grandmother is calling!

Menstruation – the dark moon phase

The inward visioning time when we release the wise blood, as well as any built up tension. Headaches, cramping, nausea and moodiness are common at this time, best relieved with some time to oneself AND engaging with the allies of the herbs, rituals, and empowered attitudes.

Let us reweave ourselves as strong women!

Let us set new boundaries, claiming time for ourselves, once a month, as we flow with life, to renew our relationship with our selves and the goddess.

HERBS TO EMPOWER WOMEN'S MOON CYCLES

These plant friends, combined for your unique needs, will heal, provide balance and strength, soften and alleviate symptoms and assist in creating elegant, empowered cycles.

Reproductive tonics

To balance, strengthen and restore natural rhythms. Often astringent, they work directly on uterine tissue to strengthen tissue and function.

Blackberry/rasberry leaf: generous in trace minerals and vitamins, including calcium. Make a tincture in apple cider vinegar to provide the perfect acidic base for effective absorption. Blackberry offers her protection when woman is vulnerable, just as she grows where the Earth has been disturbed. Allow yourself to grow a few thorns during your Moon time to create a boundary for your sacred solitude.

Nettles: a strengthening whole body tonic. Toning to the uterus, kidneys and adrenal glands. Very high in all the vitamins, trace minerals and chlorophyll. Another plant of protection, commanding respect. 'If I be waspish, best beware my sting!' She reminds us that it is our right to take some time for ourselves and, like us, she stings when she is not respected!

Vitex: In all phases of women's cycles, vitex helps to create hormonal balance. She can be ground and used as pepper in the food or tinctured. Particularly effective in issues of infertility and menopause. She increases libido in women and lowers it in men, thanks to her oestrogenic precursors. During the Middle Ages, it was given to monks to ensure they remained chaste! This is the plant that the Goddess Hera used to prepare herself for her 300 year long honeymoon with Zeus!

Lady's mantle (*Alchemilla vulgaris*): one of Brighid's totem plants, lady's mantle or Brighid's Cloak is a uterine astringent, facilitating effective menstruation and, if desired, successful implantation. The Lady wraps Her cloak around us in protection and blessing, providing sacred space on the ethereal plane when we can't go there on the physical plane. In other words, when we have our moon flow and yet we have to keep operating in the mundane realm due to jobs and other responsibilities, our lady's mantle will create the internal temple to which our spirit may descend and seek her renewal. Lady's mantle is a specific uterine tonic/astringent for all kinds of female trouble.

Emmenagogues

Herbs with this action help 'to bring on the flow'. Use in cases of congestion and late menses. The main action of these plants is *bitter*, encouraging hormonal and uterine secretion.

Mugwort: considered by our European foremothers the most sacred of plants. In addition to bringing on menses and facillitating an effective flow, mugwort also is a potent dream stimulant. Very bitter, a light infusion is usually all that is necessary. Make it your ritual drink and/or burn the dried leaf as incense to invoke the Moon Goddess and sanctify this most sacred event.

Dock: bitter, hepatic and alterative, dock provides iron, replacing what we lose in the menstrual blood. In the field, dock breaks up compacted soil; in our bodies, it helps to break up old patterns and 'stuck' energies. Dock tonifies the liver as it works hard to break down old hormones.

Lemon balm: anti-microbial, calming, uplifting nervine and emmenagogue. I've seen lemon balm work instantly many times for women experiencing late menses. Use fresh for best benefits. Also motherwort, ginger, thyme, marjoram, cinnamon, catnip or calendula.

Nervines and antispasmodics

For stretched nerves and cramps!

Crampbark: excellent as a decoction or tincture for relieving the most painful cramps and body aches. Take internally and also use externally as a liniment, applying directly to the painful area.

Clary sage: a drop of the essential oil, gently rubbed into the temples, can still all the negative mind chatter and gently lifts us out of depression. Rubbed into the site of ovarian pain, its antispasmodic action brings immediate relief. The leaves are wonderful in a ritual bath or steam. Use a light hand as too much can cause a headache.

Chamomile: a calming nervine and digestive aid, gently bitter and carminative. Use as a tea and/or use the essential oil in baths and for anointing.

Lemon balm: see emmenagogues.

Skullcap: a sedative ally for when nerves are really stretched! Skullcap will put you into deep sleep so that you can journey within and your central nervous system can be healed and strengthened. Sort of like when the Crone gives the apple to Snow White or causes Sleeping Beauty to prick her finger on the spindle. They both go to sleep as maidens (the shamanic journey) and they awaken as fully sexual women.

Flower essences

Use Bach flower essences of wild rose, larch, mustard, gorse and gentian to aid with feelings of apathy, resignation, despondency, inferiority, despair, hopelessness, discouragement, self-doubt and gloom.

Astringents

Plants with this action are very helpful in cases of excessive flow (menorrhagia) and erratic spotting (metrorrhagia). The following suggested herbs will help to regulate the cycle, without inhibiting the natural process. These have a specific affinity for the uterus and related tissue, giving strength and tone.

Lady's mantle: see tonics.

Geranium: this common field weed is also helpful for haemorrhoids and diarrhoea. Use the leaves in spring and summer; dig the rhizomes in the autumn.

Yarrow: the plant that Chiron gave to Achilles to stop the bleeding of his soldiers' wounds. Yarrow lowers blood pressure, acts as a urinary antiseptic in cases of cystitis, stimulates digestion and acts as an astringent. It is a gentle diuretic for that 'bloated' feeling and I have found its diaphoretic powers to be helpful in formulas for hot flushes and night sweats.

Demulcents

The more moist the womb, the easier the endometrium will slough off. They will help to restore the moisture balance as in cases of vaginal dryness, etc.

Marshmallow: as a tea or tincture, the root and leaf of marshmallow are supremely miosturising.

Borage: also aids the adrenal glands.

Mallow: softens and soothes the rough edges.

Chickweed.

Anti-microbials

To heal and clear reproductive infections including pelvic inflammatory disease, vaginitis, etc.

Thyme: works swiftly to clear infection and, used ritually, gives us the 'time' to journey within. Also, rosemary, sage, marjoram, garlic and yarrow.

Adaptogens

Help with stress. Feed those adrenals!

Borage
Nettles
Dandelion

Analgesics

To relieve pain.

Scullcap
Poppy

Combine with

Antispasmodics

To slow or stop smooth muscle spasms such as cramps.

Crampbark
Chamomile
Valerian
Ginger root

ACUTE CRAMP REMEDY

Tampons are the major cause of cramps and the leading cause of pelvic inflammatory diseases. Your uterus is telling you, 'get this thing out of me! It's blocking my flow!' I strongly encourage women to use pads as much as possible. Ideally, flannel pads allow us to take our consumer dollars away from the multi-national pharmaceuticals and to not contribute more garbage to the landfills and they're more comfortable. Since they're reusable, they also cost a lot less. Now! Having said that...

> Crampbark – 4 oz.
> Wood betony – 2 oz.
> Skullcap or damiana – 2 oz.

This is a dry herb recipe. If you have fresh herbs, use equal parts to fill the jar. Place in a 1 qt. Mason jar and fill with vodka, brandy, whiskey or red wine. Store in a warm, dark place and shake every day to ensure maximum extraction. After a minimum of two weeks (preferably a month), strain through muslin. Take 1–2 tsp. to relieve cramps and muscle aches, repeating dose every 20–30 minutes until pain is alleviated. Stay home and pamper yourself with hot baths and your favourite warm fuzzies!

Do NOT take this when you have to drive or be mentally sharp. If that be the case, use the following:

> Crampbark – 2 oz.
> Willow bark – 2 oz.
> Marshmallow root – 2 oz.

The first two herbs are quite astringent, so marshmallow will balance with her demulcent nature, moisturising the womb and helping everything to flow smoothly.

WOMAN POWER TEA

> Blackberry leaf – $1\frac{1}{4}$ parts
> Borage– $1\frac{1}{4}$ parts
> Nettles – $1\frac{1}{4}$ parts
> Whole dandelion – 1 part
> Rosemary – $\frac{1}{4}$ part

Make a large batch of this, using your 'handful' to equal a part. Store in a glass jar and drink 1–3 cups per day throughout your cycle to balance and strengthen, alleviating PMS from within.

MOONTHYME TEA

A calming to sedative blend

> Chamomile – $\frac{1}{2}$ part
> Nettles – 1 part
> Damiana – $\frac{1}{2}$ part

To go really deep, add 1 part skullcap. Drink 1–2 cups for relief of symptoms.

SYMPTOMS OF PMS AND APPROPRIATE REMEDIES

Cramps and pain

Cramp tincture, internal and external. Massage with clary sage/lavender essential oils. Assume the 'toad posture' to align the uterus and open and relax the pelvis. Drink moonthyme tea.

Bloating

Drink water. The more you drink, the more you'll flush. Dandelion leaf tea is an excellent diuretic and replaces potassium. Drink yarrow tea. Exercise also helps the body release excess water.

Cravings

Woman power tea. Eat some protein.

Nausea

Drink water – nausea in women's cycles is often due to dehydration. Thyme tea – 1 cup should alleviate it.

Digestive problems

Woman power tea. Water, water, water...
   Dandelion and dock tea as a digestive bitter and for constipation.
   Chamomile, meadowsweet or peppermint tea to ease symptoms.
   Aperients and laxatives relieve congestion in the pelvic region.
   Yellow dock root, dandelion root, psyllium seeds.

Depression

Often due to not getting some precious alone time. Send everyone away and take a bath, curl up with a good book or your journal, eat a little chocolate, have a good weep, take a nap, dream...
   Take 1 tsp. of St. John's wort and borage tincture and/or 4 drops of mustard flower essence, three times daily, if chronic. Seek counselling and self-empowerment activities.

Heavy bleeding

1 cup of sage tea with honey during bleeding to curtail flooding or yarrow tea, 2–3 cups a day. Woman power tea all month long to correct.
   Women experiencing flooding or break-through bleeding should avoid blood-thinning herbs such as cleavers, red clover, willow bark, pennyroyal, also aspirin, midol and large amounts of Vitamin C.

Heart palpitations

Motherwort tincture – 1 tsp. should do the trick. Take another in 20 minutes if they persist.

Insomnia

Passion flower or scullcap tea, one-half hour before bedtime.

Skin problems

Elder and calendula flower tea – drink and use as a facial toner. Cleavers, calendula, chickweed and dock tincture – equal parts, 1 tsp. 3 times per day. Water.

MAGICS TO CELEBRATE

Honour your blood

Keep a gallon jar of water in your bathroom to receive your used pads. Let them soak for a bit and then use the water to feed your gardens and give back to mother earth. (There is no finer fertiliser for your plants!)

Moon calendar

Women invented time-keeping by tracking their cycles. Lunar time was marked long before solar time. Find a good-sized bone or tree branch and carve a mark into it for each menses. Keep it on your altar. Feel the power build each month as you make your mark and bless it with your sacred blood. Do this 13 times for a full lunar year.

Belly rock

Go to a river or a creek. Contemplate her flowing and make an offering. Find a flattish rock that feels good and heavy when you lay it on your belly. Take it home and paint it with meaningful symbols – the spiral would be appropriate. When your Moonthyme comes, lay the rock in the Sun to get nice and warm, then lie down and put the rock on your belly as a natural 'heating pad'.

Moon incense

We, as the maiden, walk with the Crone, receiving Her wisdom during our Moonthyme. Burn this incense to facilitate your journey and honour your power.

Mix equal parts of mugwort, vervain, red rose petals and cedar.

Moon oil

Use this oil to anoint your body and affirm her sacredness. In 1 oz. of almond oil, add 5 drops each of the following essential oils: basil, cedar, lavender, clary sage and rose geranium; or create your own personal Moonthyme blends!

Aine incense

Aine is the Irish Maiden Goddess who, when pursued by an unwanted suitor, cast her perfume over the meadow of flowers to confuse and deter the dogs he had sent to chase her, thus escaping. Aine is an independent and intelligent young woman, using her wits and feminine power to outmanoeuvre the (patriarchal) suitor who seeks to dominate her. She remains wild and free!

> Meadowsweet flowers – $\frac{1}{2}$ cup
> Pine needles – $\frac{1}{2}$ cup
> Lemon verbena oil – 10 drops

MAIDENTHYME

(Note: Maidens are very unique individuals and I am well aware that many of today's maidens are very 'sophisticated and mature beyond their years'. The following assignations are energies of the innocence we all had before we became too jaded or cool and are certainly open to creative additions. They can be incorporated into rituals that restore lost innocence and wonder. After a painful divorce, I decorated my bedroom in soft pinks – NOT one of my usual colours – and it really helped in my healing.

Predominant element: Air.

Time: Dawn, new moon, spring, menarche, Brighid's Day.

Goddesses: Aine, Brighid, Cernal, Bloedwedd, Aurora, Core, Artemis, Diana, Pandora, Persephone, Psyche.

Powers: Beginning, initiating, questing, seeking, adventuring, discovering, amusing, laughing, playing, endearing, claiming, celebrating, dancing, imagining, trusting.

Planets and signs: Aries, Gemini, Virgo, Mercury.

Colours: shades of light – white, pale, sky-blue, spring green, soft flower pinks, sunshine yellow, moon-blood red.

Fabrics: light and airy, moving with her body. Cotton, jersey, rayon.

Animals: butterflies, hummingbirds, kittens, puppies, dolphins, sea otters, horses, fawns, cubs, unicorns.

Plants: violets, lavender, chamomile, pink roses, artemisias, sweet peas, lemon balm, meadowsweet, clary sage, primroses, thyme.

Stones: rose quartz, clear quartz, moonstone, pink tourmaline, fluorite.
Metal: silver.
Tools: feathers for magical flight; bells for calling the Fairie; a bag to hold
the magic gathered; seeds of flowers and inspiration and dreams to
be manifested; a box to hold her secrets.
Foods: seeds, nuts, raw fruits and vegetables, sandwiches, cookies, juice
(the sack lunch for a day's exploring). Red foods – apples, beets,
tomatoes, etc.

Women's wombs are the holy grail, the sacred chalice, the place from
which all life comes. I believe that if we remember and honour that
mystery, we go a long way toward reclaiming our health and our power.

THE PRAYER OF THE CHALICE

Mother,
To thee I raise my whole being,
A vessel emptied of self.

Accept, Lady,
This, my emptiness,
And so fill me with Thyself,
Thy light, Thy Love, Thy Life,
That these Thy precious gifts
May radiate through me and overflow
The chalice of my heart
Into the hearts of all with whom
I come in contact this day
Revealing unto them
The beauty of Thy Joy and Wholeness
And the serenity of Thy Peace
Which nothing can destroy!

(Engraved on a sacred well in Wales)

THE WARRIOR QUEEN

The Warrior Goddess

Goddesses: Artemis, Diana, Brighid, Boudicea, Kali, Grainne, Joan of
Arc, Harriet Tubman, Epona, Hippolyta, Banba, Maeve, Macha,

Cartimandua, Scotia, Athena, the Morrigan, Women surviving everywhere.

Powers: activating, protecting, guarding, shielding, waiting, listening, tracking, seeking, finding, freeing, taming, honouring, respecting, discovering, exploring, dancing, silence, invisibility.

Birthing: the original warrior act: the ultimate vision quest.

Qualities/concepts

Courage, justice, determination, truth, geis, strength, stamina, flexibility, defence, protection, swiftness, silence, invisibility, wit, wisdom, tools.

Dragon medicine: yelling, raging (at injustice), truth-speaking, adventuring, risking, sacrificing, strengthening, encouraging, energising, piercing, reaching

Place: the south, mountain tops, the desert, arenas, the wilderness.

Planets and signs: Mars, Aries etc.

Colours: red, orange, yellow, white, camouflage, gold, black (for Moon Warriors).

Animals: predators such as the falcon, the hawk, the eagle, the raven, wildcats, the wolf, wild boar, the dragon, the horse.

Plants: borage, rosemary, dragon's blood, dandelion, nettles, mullein, yarrow, horsetail, basil, blackberry, raspberry, calendula, rue, garlic, thyme, St. John's wort, High John the Conqueror.

Stones: carnelian, bloodstone, haematite, fire agate.

Tools: the knife for cutting arrows, building shelters; the compass for direction; the spear aimed straight at the goal; the sword of truth and justice; the wand a torch in the dark; the shield of personal honour and protection; the cloak for disguise, invisibility, protection; the headband to keep her mindful; tattoos and scars as marks of achievement; recordings of experience.

HERBS OF PROTECTION

Rosemary: provides clear thinking in the midst of conflict. Instils respect in the adversary. Maintains calm in crisis.

Borage: strengthens the heart and instils courage. Nurtures the adrenal glands for accurate adrenaline secretion.

Blackberry: to establish and maintain boundaries. Protector of Mother Earth and her children.

St. John's wort: carry into court to ensure justice is done. Can also use
   High John the Conqueror.
Rose: relaxes the negative ego (fear/anger) to understand the truth of
   what is going on. Alleviates worry and useless paranoia.
Wormwood: the Moon Warrior. Facilitates creative resolution to
   conflicts and problems.
Dragon's blood: engages the protection of the dragon. Intensifies what-
   ever it is combined with.
Salt: Creates boundaries and protects.
Frankincense: restores sacredness. Cleanses and purifies.
Myrrh: see frankincense.
Vervain: protects from negativity, including our own!

SOME TRADITIONAL RECIPES

Fiery wall of protection

Dragon's blood, frankincense, myrrh, salt.

Uncrossing powder

Lavendar, rose petals, bay leaves, vervain.

Banishing

Bay leaves, yarrow, rose petals, myrrh, salt.

WARRIOR WOMAN

Bold and daring. Thriving on challenge. She keeps herself fit and knows
how to pace herself.

   Practising acute observation, she battles injustice, oppression and her
own limitations. Standing centred in the midst of chaos.

   Dependable and focused, she wields the sword of her mind. Self-
contained and thoroughly independent, she is the high-minded seeker
of her own path.

   Tough, yet flexible, she is the protector of wild nature.

   Strong, silent and confident enough to be invisible, her enemies are the
instruments of her transformation.

   She knows when to be still and when to act. She is willing to walk
against the flow of society with an attitude of courage and faith.

She battles her personal demons to win freedom from all personal, social and cultural hindrances.

She is a warrioress of the heart and of the spirit; courageously feeling, loving, experiencing all aspects of her self and life, waging war on any limitations of her full self-expression. She accepts, encourages and supports others in their own empowerment... with kindness and consideration.

A woman would do well to train as a warrior before she becomes a lover. Indeed, this is how it was done in ancient cultures. Warrior training ensures that she has healthy boundaries, healthy self-esteem, that she always acts from and requires truth, honour and mutual respect. She learns to be empowering and ennobling in her relationships and is always able to stand on her own two feet. She guards the sanctity of the Spirit in all things and stands for the personal freedom and free choice of all the Mother's children. She seeks adventure and embraces challenge in her personal growth. She is more patient than all her enemies and is ultimately triumphant. She dances to the rhythms of her life with flaming passion and graceful strength. She never swerves from her purpose, aiming straight toward her goals. Her Sword of Truth hunts out and cuts away oppression, deception, dis-ease. The Shield of her strengths recounts her brave deeds and protects her from those who would wound her. She is Virgin – belonging only to herself in this cycle of self-discovery. Once she knows Who She Is, then she is empowered enough, whole enough, and wise enough to share herself in intimate, equitable, satisfying relationship.

She is committed to physical, emotional, mental and spiritual fitness, honouring her body with healthy exercise and nourishing foods. She knows when she can push herself and when to retreat and take her rest.

She is a trailblazer, a scout, and a pioneer, a dragon-rider and ignorance-slayer. She is a torch in the darkness, the storm that cleanses, the fire that transforms creative thought into action and manifestation.

She has rid herself of all excess baggage and travels lightly towards her destination, studying the signs and portents of Nature for clues to her next steps.

She risks the status quo and sacrifices complacency in order to grow.

We women are our own worst enemy as a result of the fear and loathing of Feminine Power present in the world today. When we believe in 'lack', that there is only so much to go around, we betray each other. We compete with each other; we compare ourselves negatively to each other. We force ourselves into linear modalities, forgetting we are cyclic creatures. We become isolated, cut off from each other,

Nature, our bodies, our feelings, and our power. Where is our pride? Our confidence? Our loyalty to our personal well being and that of our sisters? I believe that breast and reproductive cancers, P.I.D., infertility, PMS, and vaginal infections are all too often physical manifestations of the self-loathing we feel for our female selves.

Who is your Warrior Woman self?
What is her name?
What is her style?
What are her tools of defence?
What are her powers?
What is her geiss? Your sacred obligation?
To what will you dedicate those powers and tools in the coming year?
How will you nourish and activate those powers?

A chant for the protection of our children, our Mother, the Earth and their future

Mistress of Magic, enchantments deep
You who beckon to fallen heroes
Harken to this your child!
I would weave strong magic for protection
Deep magic to bind and chasten
I repel all attackers!
Beware! Foul troublemakers!
For Freya whispers her spells in my ear!
Freya, Queen of the Valkyrie, stands at my side!

MOTHERTHYME

Herbal care for pregnancy and childbirth

Let us invoke Brighid as the Sacred Midwife to bless this work ...

Woman giving birth is the original shamanic journey,
The most sacred of acts,
The most wonderful of miracles.
She is
The most awesome of Warriors,
The holy gateway between Heaven and Earth!

Pregnancy begins at the moment of conception. A woman who chooses to bear a child should be aware of the power and holiness of her body during this time. Birth has, since ancient times, been an act of power, an act of transformation, a primal, natural thing. In today's hospital environment, that power has been greatly diminished – women are treated as weak, unable to deliver without machines and drugs. Caesareans occur at an alarming rate.

We need to reclaim the sacredness of giving birth. We need to accord women the awe and respect they deserve for creating Life. Honouring the Mother is at the core of how our world can and will be healed. Ancient matri-focal cultures concentrated on supporting and caring for all mothers and their children. This, of course, ensured that every member of the community was taken care of, since everyone was the child of a mother!

Herbs are wonderful allies for empowering a woman during pregnancy, labour and delivery. They have accompanied women on this most holy of shamanic journeys since the beginning of time. While certain herbs should not be used during pregnancy, there are many that offer great nutrient and gentle healing actions, with no fear of harm.

I could list hundreds of herbs that a woman should not use during pregnancy and some would surely be overlooked. Herbs with alkaloids, coumarins or strong essential oils should not be used. We will focus on the herbs that may be used safely.

HERBS FOR PREGNANCY

Nettles
Raspberry/blackberry
Dandelion
Chickweed
Meadowsweet
Leaves and fruits of the *Rosaceae* family, including rose, apple, peach,
    cherry, plum, and strawberry
Lady's mantle
Mallow
Marshmallow
Oatstraw
Rose hips
Cornsilk

Look for alkaloid-free, vitamin and mineral-rich herbs that are high in flavanoids.

STRONG BEAUTIFUL MOTHER TONIC

3 oz. Raspberry or blackberry leaf – tones and strengthens the uterus. High in calcium and flavanoids.

3 oz. Nettles – provides all the vitamins and trace minerals, including folic acid!

2 oz. Dandelion leaf and root – tones and strengthens the urinary system and liver. Prevents oedema (water retention)

2 oz. Oatstraw – provides additional calcium. Tones and strengthens the nervous system and promotes strong bones in mother and baby.

8 oz. Total mixed dried herbs. Add 1 tsp. per cup of boiling water and steep for 20 minutes. Strain and drink 3 cups a day.

NAUSEA/MORNING SICKNESS

Avoid large meals and/or long stretches between meals. A lack of Vitamin B is often the cause. Incorporate Vitamin B rich foods into the diet.

Avocado
Bananas
Dried plums
Lentils
Molasses
Peas
Skimmed milk
Sunflower seeds
Tuna
Wheat germ
White chicken
Whole grains

Plants high in flavanoids can counter nausea. Drinking the 'Beautiful Mother' tonic, in most cases, will prevent or alleviate nausea. In addition, peach leaf and meadowsweet can help. Eat yoghurt and kefir for beneficial bacteria.

VARICOSE VEINS

A lack of bioflavanoids and Vitamin C can lead to a sluggish circulatory system and/or weak blood vessels. The 'Beautiful Mother' tea is rich in

bioflavanoids as are buckwheat, whole grains and citrus fruits. Addition-
ally, add 1–2 cups of rose hip tea to the daily rituals.

STRONG VESSEL LINAMENT

Make an apple cider vinegar tincture of equal parts yarrow, comfrey and
nettles. Apply to legs daily in an upward motion toward the heart.
Elevate and massage legs as often as possible.

MOTHER BELLY OIL

For supple skin and the prevention of stretch marks.

$\frac{1}{4}$ cup cocoa butter
$\frac{1}{2}$ cup coconut oil
$\frac{1}{2}$ cup apricot kernel oil

Heat ingredients together gently until the cocoa butter is melted. Whisk
for 2 minutes when cooled to room temperature. Store in a jar in the
fridge and apply daily.

CONSTIPATION

Take 1 tsp. psyllium seeds added to $\frac{1}{4}$ cup of fruit juice in the morning,
followed by 1–2 glasses of water. Psyllium seed is very demulcent and
will facilitate a normal bowel movement by the next morning, deeply
cleansing the intestinal tract along the way.

Eat lots of greens and whole grains.

Drink a total of two quarts of water and herb tea a day.

Exercise – especially walking and stretching.

DIARRHOEA

Eat apple sauce with $\frac{1}{4}$ tsp. cinnamon. The apple sauce cleanses the intestinal tract quickly and the anti-microbial action of the cinnamon deals
with the bacteria that's causing the diarrhoea.

Drink plenty of fluids to prevent dehydration.

HAEMORRHOIDS

Apply witch hazel and lavender compresses.
  Follow with comfrey, yarrow and plantain salve.
  Do Kegal exercises to strengthen muscles and blood vessels.
  Avoid spicy foods, which seem to increase irritation.

INSOMNIA

Drink a cup of oatstraw tea or a glass of warm milk.
  Meditate – focus on breathing and relaxing each part of the body, starting with the toes and working up. Send loving affirmations to the baby.

FATIGUE

Can be due to poor nutrition and lack of Vitamin B. To the daily diet, add dried apricots, yoghurt and kefir, and vegetable juices. See morning sickness above.
  Energy is naturally more inward as the baby is growing and developing. Rest and relax!

COLDS AND FLUS

Take 1 cup of hot honegar or elder tea with lemon and honey up to three times a day. Take warm baths and go to bed!

LABOUR AND DELIVERY

To ease labour, sip nettle and raspberry tea with 10 drops angelica tincture per cup between contractions.

FOR STALLED LABOUR

Offer 20 drops angelica tincture and 20 drops wood betony in 1 cup of water.
  Have the mother breathe into a warm, wet washcloth to which 3 drops of spikenard essential oil have been applied. This really works! I once

walked into a hospital birthing room where my friend Pam was labouring to deliver her son, Ben. She was curled up in a foetal position, surrounded by many nurses (she is one herself) and there was a gloomy energy of fear and concern in the room. I asked someone what was going on and was told that she was being prepared for a Caesarean, as she wasn't progressing. I wet a washcloth in the bathroom sink, applied the spikenard oil and pushed my way through the nurses. I had a right to – I was Pam's birth coach. I held the washcloth over Pam's nose and guided her breathing in a slow, deep rhythm. I began to call the baby Ben's spirit to come and be born; his Mama needed him to come now! Then I had Pam breathe the 'Dragon Breath', doing it along with her. Within 20 minutes, she had dilated to 10 centimetres and Ben was born! All thanks to the beautiful spikenard!

Have the Mother walk, especially up and down stairs.

Relaxation is key! Play soft music, offer massage, and facilitate a guided meditation.

Clear all distractions – that includes people! Too many observers and too many energies can dilute the power of the birthing woman.

PAINFUL LABOUR/CONTRACTIONS

Offer a tea or tincture of equal parts skullcap, motherwort and catnip.

Encourage open-mouthed yelling, keeping the tone very low. Breathe in through the nose and exhale with a low roar through the mouth – what I call the Dragon Breath!

TO CALM AND GROUND THOSE IN ATTENDANCE

Rescue remedy.

Spell each other – minimise distractions

Drink nutrient, bitter teas for energy and stamina.

LABOUR MASSAGE OIL

14 drops clary sage essential oil

5 drops rose geranium essential oil

6 drops lavender essential oil
in 2 oz. almond oil

TO AVOID AND/OR HEAL PERINEUM TEARS

Do Kegal exercises throughout pregnancy.

During the eighth month of pregnancy, massage the perineum with olive oil.

Take sitz baths with comfrey, yarrow and lavender tea.

Apply comfrey/lavender salve.

AFTER BIRTH

To help expel placenta

Breast-feeding.
Raspberry tea throughout pregnancy and labour.
1 tsp. Angelica tincture in $\frac{1}{4}$ cup water.
Massage uterus.
A glass of red wine.
Squat in a 'frog' position.

The cord

To disinfect and aid healing apply honey or comfrey salve with lavender essential oil or Vitamin E oil at each diaper change.

AFTER BIRTH TEA

To tone and return uterus to normal size, provide deep nourishment to the mother and rich milk for the baby.

1 oz. nettles
1 oz. oatstraw
1 oz. blackberry
1 oz. fennel
4 oz. total dried herb

Mix together and store in a jar. Mother should drink 3–4 cups a day and can continue through breast-feeding. If there was haemorrhage during labour, add an equal part of yarrow for 1 week.

HERBS FOR BIRTH BLESSINGS

To bless the mother on this, the most wondrous and sacred of journeys. In today's modern societies, there is no honouring or blessing for the mother. The rituals of birth have been distilled down to the baby shower. I want to encourage the restoration of the birth blessing, focusing on the mother as she prepares to labour and deliver and the baby blessing, occurring after the birth when the new one is actually present to receive gifts and good wishes!

The following herbs have been incorporated into birth and baby blessings since ancient times. Craft these allies into incenses, anointing oils, blessing waters and altar offerings. Use a light hand – do not offer for use internally or in baths during pregnancy, unless otherwise specified.

Basil – to invoke the power and magic of the Dragon to strengthen and protect mother and child. Bestows Peace and Plenty.

Dandelion – beloved by Brighid, the Sacred Midwife. Gives the strength of the Lioness to the labouring woman and gives the blessings of the Sun – self-esteem, success in Life, dreams manifested. Dandelion can be taken as a tea throughout pregnancy.

Blackberry – also much beloved by Brighid. The leaf can be used as a nutritive and uterine strengthening tea, burned as incense, added to the bath. The fruit can be drunk as juice or eaten plain or added to all sorts of wonderful recipes. Bestows tenacity and determination and prosperity. Safe for internal use throughout pregnancy.

Borage – gives courage and power to the Warrior Mother.

Sage – gives wisdom and grounding.

Rose – nurtures the heart and bestows the blessings of Love on all concerned.

Rosemary – offers protection and respect to the mother.

Mugwort – the 'midwife' herb. Mugwort bestows the blessings of the Moon on the mother and the child. Burn as incense to ensure a safe and easy delivery.

SPELLS AND RITUALS

During pregnancy

The contemplation of shells and flowers is a powerful reflection of the vaginal opening, the sacred gateway through which the baby will be born.

A poppet can be made to represent the baby, filling it with herbs and other magical things to represent various blessings. This ritual can involve the whole family.

Birth blessing

Invite the mother's support circle to gather, asking them to bring a beautiful bead and a gift of power for the mother. Prepare a ritual bath. Do not use essential oils this time. Float flower petals in the water instead. Let the mother steep in the blessings, then let her dress in a lovely, flowing garment. Lead her out from the bath through a double line of attendees, who affirm her beauty and power as she walks through. Guide her into the centre and then have attendees make a circle around her. Invoke and give the blessings of the four elements and Brighid, the sacred Midwife. Individuals can each take an element and be responsible for research, meditation and crafting of a blessing. When these have been given, then some beading string can be passed around the circle, each participant naming a blessing that they are adding to the necklace, represented by their bead. Present the finished necklace to the mother, thank the Elements and Brighid and open the circle for gift-giving and feasting.

During labour

The mother and/or members of her support circle can invoke the blessings of the Elements at the four corners of the house or hospital room – Air at the East, Fire at the South and so on. Physical blessings – incense for Air, a candle for Fire, etc. – may be used or, if in a hospital, where they may be frowned upon, simply work with energy and intent.

QUEENTHYME – CRONETHYME

A celebration of menopause

Old Woman, Old Friend, Ancient Mother, Grand One, She who can comfort with a touch, heal or destroy with a gaze, She who leads us to the magical realms to aid us in our Spirit's rebirth.

Comfortable in the dark, She sits alone, spinning and weaving magic and dreams and Life and Death. She is not lonely; She is alone, Al-one with Her divine power in the Universe. Darkness to Her is the rich, fertile soil, nourishing strong, healthy roots, the foundation of a rich, healthy life.

Darkness is depth and rest and moonbeams and starlight. Dark and deep are Her colours; the colours of night-time lit by the hearthfire, deep royal purple proclaims Her Queen of Night and Moon and Magic, the Moon-blood red of Woman announces Her as Priestess of the Blood Mysteries, Keeper of the sacred temple of the Goddess, guardian of the sanctity of Woman. She preserves plants and foods and traditions.

Considered by healthy cultures as the spiritual head of the family, She spins and weaves and cuts the tapestry of the seasons, keeping the Holy Days. She weaves a web of connectedness between self and family, community and Nature, to the Divine in life. She holds the focus, while allowing and encouraging self-expression.

She no longer releases Her wise-blood once a Moon, but holds it within Her, building in wisdom and power. She is Her own authority, sharing Her experience for the ennoblement and empowerment of others.

Traditionally, historically, her family and community revered menopausal woman. Freed from the responsibilities of birthing and raising children, She becomes midwife to the generations, aiding physical and spiritual birth. She knows the deep, dark places of the soul.

Witch Queen of the Underworld, Lady of the Night, She absorbs our hurts and sorrows into Her solitary darkness, healing and transforming them into stars of light. She comforts the dying and leads them to their rest. Her guiding spirit illuminates the way. She buries, composts and recycles all things. She banishes fear and negativity.

Her beauty does not fade, merely changes.

She wears the mantle of Power gracefully.

CRONETHYME

Time – midnight, dark moon, winter, Samhain, menopause, second Saturn return.

Place – the north, caves, deep woods, elder trees, standing stones, crossroads, barrows, cemeteries, compost piles.

Predominant element – Earth.

Goddesses – Caille, Cailleagh na Mointeach, Eire, Cerridwen, Danu, Aine, Domnu, Scotia, Shiela-na-Gig, Skadi, Ragnell, Spider Grandmother.

Powers – midwifing birth and death, spinning, weaving, healing, teaching, chronicling, counselling, guiding, divination and prophesy, brewing, burying, banishing, dissolving, leading, directing, completing, ending, cutting, carving, travelling, recycling, composting.

Planets and signs – Scorpio, Capricorn, Pisces, Saturn, Neptune, Pluto.

Colours – dark and deep, reflective of light, black, forest green, lapis blue, blood red, royal purple, silver to thunder cloud grey.

Herbs – sage, nettles, mugwort, elder, vitex, garlic, anise, cloves, juniper berries, belladonna*, thornapple*, poppy, hemlock* foxglove*, mushrooms*.

(*Warning – poisonous! – do not ingest!)

Animals – raven, crow, owl, turkey vulture, bat, spider, black cats and dogs, snake, mouse, dragon, phoenix, black hens, toads.

Stones and crystals – smoky quartz, onyx, obsidian, garnet, black pearls, haematite, diamond, clear quartz, rocks, fossils, salt.

Fabrics – like the night sky, studded with stars, velvet, brocades, soft wools and wovens, lace.

Tools – knife to cut the pain of birth, the cord of life; to carve sacred space; scissors to cut the fabric of life; cauldron to brew magic and regeneration; wand – the extension of her will; staff – symbol of authority, announces Her presence; veils to guard her sanctity, the robes of nobility; runes, cards, etc. to divine the future; rocks, bones, roots, fossils, cobwebs.

Foods – underground foods – potatoes, parsnips, beets, carrots, turnips, etc. Pomegranates, apples, mushrooms, black berries, red and berry wines, tea.

CRONETHYME – THE EMPOWERMENT OF MENOPAUSE

Menopause is an achievement, not an illness!

It is a Rite of Passage that marks the entry into a cycle of Life that can honour one's experiences and the wisdom gathered from them.

An opportunity to 'change', a metamorphosis, it is a natural process requiring natural methods for empowerment. It is estimated that there will be 50 million menopausal women in the United States by 2013 and that spells a lot of dollars for the multi-national drug corporations if they convince us we're sick and need all their pills. They don't want us to know that, with herbs, nutrition, exercise and vision questing, we can create an easy and powerful transition into another sacred cycle of life. Menopause is a time to break rules, dream new dreams and revision ourselves as Women of Power, Women of Experience! The multinationals certainly don't want that!

Due in most part, I think, to the negative attitudes toward ageing in this country, there are symptoms of imbalance that can arise. Our bodies send out signals to communicate their changing needs, which can be easily addressed with natural, inexpensive herbs and lifestyle and attitude adjustments.

THE SYMPTOMS OF IMBALANCE

Hot flushes and night sweats – there is an emerging school of thought that hot flushes or 'power surges' are actually good for us, that they actually providing metabolic cleansing, cleaning up old cells and free radicals that are precursors to cancer. Therefore, when we suppress or avoid them through hormone replacement therapy, we are actually diminishing our ability to fend off disease!

Insomnia
Lack of sexual interest
Depression
Menstrual flooding
Irritability
Heart palpitations
Skin and vaginal dryness
Osteoporosis
Diminished energy

POSSIBLE CAUSES

Poor nutrition
Lack of exercise
Stress
Hormone imbalance
Thyroid imbalance
Poor absorption of nutrients
Vitamin B deficiency
Attitude

CONTRAINDICATIONS TO HORMONE REPLACEMENT THERAPY

Any woman who is experiencing or has a history of any of the following should not take HRT.

Breast or uterine cancer
Diabetes
Migraines
Serious high blood pressure
Liver diseases
History of blood clots
Uterine fibroids
History of stroke
Gall bladder disease or gallstones
Varicose veins
Fibrocystic breasts
Endometrial cancer
Obesity

ADVANTAGES OF HRT

Elimination of hot flushes
Elimination of vaginal dryness
Initial decrease of bone loss

DISADVANTAGES OF HRT

Increase in fibroid growth
Increased risk of stroke
Increased risk of breast cancer
Increased risk of gall bladder disease
More medical expenses and visits
Monthly menses can continue
Decreased folic acid levels
Water retention
Breast soreness
Mood swings

CHOOSING ANOTHER ROAD

Food therapy

Create a nutritional programme that is high in fibre and protein, low in fat, dairy and carbohydrates.

Cut down/delete refined foods, sugar, caffeine, alcohol, carbonated drinks, especially 'diet'.

Include 'friendly' bacteria foods – yoghurt, kefir, etc.

Include vegetable proteins, nuts, whole grains, vegetables and vegetable juices for vitamins and minerals.

Include 5 servings a day of the following calcium rich foods to prevent osteoporosis – combine with acidic foods and dressings (lemons, tomatoes, apple cider vinegar) to promote absorption.

Cooked Greens

Broccoli, mustard, greens, collards, kale, lambs quarters.

Nettles – 3 tablespoons of nettle/apple cider vinegar tincture a day will provide the equivalent of 5 servings! Do eat whole veggies for fibre as well!

Other

Seaweeds, dried fruits, blackstrap molasses, corn tortillas.

Herbal vinegars

Calcium-high herbs steeped in apple cider vinegar to increase absorption – the perfect supplement!

Fresh nettles
Fresh dandelion
Dried comfrey leaf
Fresh chickweed

Use as a condiment or take as honegar – mix 1 tsp. of the infused vinegar with 1 tsp. honey and 8 oz. water and take 3 glasses a day. Each tsp. of herbal vinegar can be considered the equivalent of one of those servings of vegetables!

Oestrogen-promoting foods and herbs

Meat, cheese, eggs, yogurt, apples, carrots, tomatoes, cherries, yams, potatoes, olives, peanuts, eggplant, plums, food yeast, raspberry fruit and leaf, wheat germ, garlic, anise seed, fennel, parsley, pepper, sage, oregano, alfalfa, cereal grains (except rye, buckwheat or white rice),

BODYWORK

Use it or lose it!

- Weight-bearing exercise – prevents/reverses osteoporosis.
- Yoga – promotes flexibility, balances energy.
- Dance – promotes flexibility, improves cardio-vascular and circulatory health, channels self-expression.
- Martial arts – promotes flexibility, increases self-confidence and strength.
- Massage – promotes endocrine/lymphatic health, aids circulation, increases well-being. We need to be touched!

161

WEAVING THE WEB

Suggestions for working with Lunathyme and the lessons of this chapter

Contemplate your own relationship and experience of women and women's cycles.

What are the empowering rituals and attitudes that you already practise?

Are there other things you might do to more deeply empower and honour the Sacred Feminine?

Create a tea, an incense and a bath blend for each of the cycles, pertinent to your specific needs and those of women you know. Experience them all yourself, so you'll have a direct experience when you give them to other women.

Create a blessing ritual for a woman you know. Create a blessing ritual for your Self!

Create your personal mythology of your menstrual journey. Who are you at the core of your being? What are the fears you must face, the blocks you must dissolve, the tension you must release? Who are you going to meet, there in the Womb Cave? What does She have to say?

Work with the three herbs of the Materia Medica. Record your experiences.

BRIGHID'S BLESSINGS
ON ALL WOMEN AND THEIR CHILDREN!

CHAPTER 8

REPRODUCTIVE HEALTH – MEN

THE WARRIOR

Qualities/concepts

Courage, justice, determination, truth, geis, strength, stamina, flexibility, defence, protection, swiftness, silence, invisibility, wit, wisdom, tools.

Deities and heroes: Lugh, the many-skilled one, Dagda, the Good Father, Finn McCool, Brian Boru, Paidraig Pearse, James Connelly, Wolf Tone, Daniel O'Connel.

Powers: activating, protecting, guarding, shielding, waiting, listening, tracking, seeking, finding, freeing, taming, honouring, respecting, discovering, exploring, dancing, silence, invisibility.

Dragon medicine: truth-speaking, adventuring, risking, sacrificing, strengthening, encouraging, energising, piercing, reaching.

Place: the south, mountain tops, the desert, arenas, the wilderness.

Planets and signs: Mars, Aries.

Colours: red, orange, yellow, white, camouflage, gold, black (for moon warriors).

Animals: predators: the falcon, the hawk, the eagle, the raven, wildcats, the wolf, wild boar, the dragon, the horse.

Plants: borage, rosemary, dragon's blood, dandelion, nettles, mullein, yarrow, horsetail, basil, blackberry, raspberry, calendula, rue, garlic, thyme, St. John's wort, High John the Conqueror.

Stones: Carnelian, bloodstone, haematite, fire agate, obsidian.

Tools: The knife for cutting arrows, building shelters. The compass for direction. The spear aimed straight at the goal. The sword of truth and justice. The wand, a torch in the dark. The shield of personal honour and protection. The cloak for disguise, invisibility, protection. The headband to keep mindful. Tattoos and scars. Marks of achievement; recordings of experience.

Herbs of immunity

Thyme garlic yarrow cayenne onion calendula cleavers.
St. John's wort, elecampane, Oregon grape, echinecea essential oils.

Being a warrior is NOT about:

> Attacking.
> Dominating.
> Being harsh or insensitive (loud).
> Being aggressive or self-righteous.
> Self-aggrandisement.
> Feeling more entitled than others.

Negative emotion can be channelled into positive action.

> Guilt is the energy to make change within ourselves.
> Discontent is the energy to make change for the better.
> Fear is the energy to do your best in a new situation.
> Grief is the energy that leads to deeper compassion.
> Anger is the energy to make change in the world.

Whenever we are behaving as a victim, we are manipulating, using our past to justify who we are now. We argue for our limitations to keep from changing. (I can't help it; I'm that way because...). Our negative ego is constantly trying to drag us into the past or the future. It has no respect for us. It teaches separateness.

Negative ego styles and disguises

The victim, the martyr, the struggler, the ego pamperer/enabler, the silent competitor, the rescuer, the saviour.

The weaker we are, the more inclined we are to do harm.

The ultimate battle is between our faith in the universe and our ego's cynicism, its sense of failure.

THE WARRIOR'S CODE

Consider and accept responsibility for the impact you have on other's lives – which includes your moods.

Live in accordance with the highest integrity, aligned with the heart's wisdom, inspiring others by example.

Keep your agreements – every time you break an agreement, you give power to your negative ego. It says, 'See, I told you so, you can't be counted on, you can't be trusted. This is why I have to run the show'.

Initiate and nurture the following virtues in your life:

1. Fortitude – the strength of mind and the courage to persevere in the face of adversity. The ability to 'hang in there'.
2. Temperance – self-discipline. The control of unruly passions and desires. Not indulging in things that do not serve.
3. Providence – practical wisdom. The ability to make the right choice in any situation.
4. Justice – fairness, honesty, lawfulness (of Nature and Spirit). The ability to keep one's promises.
5. Faith – choosing to believe, especially when it is most difficult and challenging.
6. Hope – maintaining an optimistic viewpoint.
7. Charity – sharing abundance with others – giving a hand to those in need.
8. Responsibility – integrity in action. The ability to respond. Responsibility is a choice.

Only those who live what they talk about can speak with true spiritual authority.

Ambition – to strive to be our best. The desire to develop and actualise our gifts.

Elegance – the greatest result produced by the least amount of effort.

Divinity – your relationship to God/dess.

Morality – is not hurting yourself or others.

It's time to shift into Warrior mode when you feel your negative ego pulling you down into the darker canyons of the Underworld.

Warning signs

Anger	Resentment	Lack of trust
Confusion	Feelings of rejection	Excessive demands
Controlling behaviour	Frustration	Overwhelm
Exhaustion	Hopelessness	Passivity
Feelings of	Insecurity	Withholding
abandonment	Jealousy	Worry

165

The 20-minute change-your-attitude exercise

First 5 minutes – recognise it.
Second 5 minutes – acknowledge it.
Third 5 minutes – forgive it.
Fourth 5 minutes – change it.

RISK! Risk complacency, the status quo. Risk going against 'the pack' and going to the beat of your own drum. Risking nothing is actually risking everything.

Men should have Rites of Passage Rituals at certain times of their lives, just as women should. The times when boys step into manhood and when men become fathers and elders are especially important. There should be a time of isolation and introspection, followed by acknowledgement and celebration by the community. Mentoring of boys and young men is vital and yet is sadly lacking in today's societies. This is an area where men could be extremely valuable and contribute greatly by passing on their wisdom and disciplines to young boys in need of role models.

RITE OF PASSAGE FOR A BOY ENTERING MANHOOD

The boy should spend time with the men of his community, be there one or many, learning of their disciplines, skills and perspectives and honing his own.

At the appropriate time, let the boy go on a vision quest, bidding farewell to the community as the boy he was. Let his boy-hair be cut away so that the new man-power can grow in. He should spend a period of time in solitude, fasting and praying. Let him seek an animal ally and a Spirit name and meditate on his Geis or personal Code of Honour. When he feels complete, let him return to the community and be welcomed as a man.

Let the blessings of the Elements be bestowed upon him. Let his family and friends gift him with symbols of empowerment for his manhood. Let him state his Personal Code of Honour to the community. He may want to signify his new manhood with a tattoo or piercing or mode of dress.

Include his favourite music, dance and foods in the celebration.

MALE REPRODUCTIVE

Essential anatomy and physiology

Covered by thin loose skin, the penis consists of an attached root, a free shaft, and an enlarged tip. It deposits sperm into the female reproductive tract and acts as the terminal duct for urination.

Internally, the penile shaft consists of three columns of erectile tissue bound together by heavy fibrous tissue. Two corpora cavernosa form the major part of the penis. On the underside, the corpus spongiosum encases the urethra. The enlarged end forms the glans penis.

The glans penis is formed from the corpus spongiosum. It is highly sensitive to sexual stimulation. The urethral meatus opens through the glans to allow urination and ejaculation.

The scrotum is an extra-abdominal pouch consisting of a thin layer of skin overlying a tighter muscle-like layer. Internally divided by a septum into two sacs, each containing a testis, an epididymis and a spermatic cord. The spermatic cord is a connective tissue sheath that encases autonomic nerve fibres, blood vessels, lymph vessels, and the vas deferens.

The testes are located in the scrotum, one in each sac, suspended outside the body cavity behind the penis. They are three degrees cooler than the rest of the body, and shaped like an egg. Each testis is surrounded by two layers of connective tissue, the tunica vaginalis (the outer layer) and a tough, whitish membrane called the tunica albuginea (the inner layer) which covers the testicle and enters the gland to form the many septa. The septa divide it into sections or lobules, which consist of a narrow, long and coiled tubule, 750 feet long, which forms the bulk of testicular tissue mass.

Testes function

Androgens (male sex hormones) are produced by the testes and the adrenals: leutenising hormone (interstitial cell-stimulating hormone) and FSH – both directly affecting the secretion of testosterone.

Testosterone is responsible for development and maintenance of male sex organs and secondary sexual characteristics, such as facial hair and vocal cord thickness. Secretion begins about two months after conception. Required for spermatogenesis.

Spermatogenesis – Sperm are produced at a rate of 500 million in the tubules of each testicle each day. These sperm cells are the smallest and most highly specialised of all the cells in the human body. They remain viable for up to 48 hours after ejaculation, up to 4 days in the reproductive tract.

Before puberty – mitosis – two daughter cells, each complete.

Puberty – Secretion of gonadotropins occurs, stimulating testes function and testosterone secretion.

FSH produces two daughter cells of which one remains spermatogonium and the other forms primary spermatocyte – undergo meiosis (2

cell divisions occur) – 4 daughter cells – spermatids – develop into spermatids – develop into spermatozoa containing $\frac{1}{2}$ genetic material and $\frac{1}{2}$
(23) chromosomes of other cells.

The duct system

Epididymis – single and tightly coiled tube 20 feet long – lies along top
and behind testes. Sperm mature and develop their ability to swim as they
pass through, on their way to the vas deferens.

Ductus or vas deferens – The tube that permits sperm to exit from
epididymis and pass from the scrotal sac into abdominal cavity. Thick,
smooth and very muscular, it can be felt or 'palpapted' through the
skin of the scrotal wall.

Extends over the top and down the posterior surface of the bladder.
The enlarged portion, the ampulla, joins the duct from the seminal
vesicle to form the ejaculatory duct. It then passes through the prostate
and permits sperm to enter into the urethra for ejaculation.

Accessory reproductive glands

Seminal vesicles (2) are pouch-like glands at the base of the bladder. They
contribute 60% of seminal fluid – yellowish, thick, rich in fructose – give
sperm energy.

Cowper's Glands are located inferior to the prostate. Secrete 10% of
the seminal fluid.

The prostate is a walnut-sized gland lying underneath the bladder and
surrounding the urethra. It continuously secretes the thin, milky, alkaline
prostatic fluid, which adds volume to the semen. It enhances sperm moti-
lity and neutralises the acidity of the urethra and the woman's vagina.

Semen is an alkaline, viscous, white secretion, consisting of sperm and
secretions of supportive sex glands.

MALE REPRODUCTIVE TONICS

Saw palmetto, yarrow, oats, burdock, dock, marshmallow root.
Urinary/prostate tonics – saw palmetto, dandelion, yarrow, burdock,
    corn silk.
Diuretics – see above.
Circulatory – yarrow, oat, hawthorn.
Alterative – yarrow, dock, burdock, nettles.
Nervines – borage, oats, lemon balm, St. John's wort, saw palmetto.

Anti-inflammatories – yarrow, thyme.

Anti-microbials – thyme, yarrow, spaghetti herbs.

Lymphatics – calendula, cleavers, apple cider vinegar.

Burdock (*Arctium lappa*) all parts – all skin conditions – seed and leaf for scrotal eczema – use powdered externally. Prostatitis and epidimytis – internally. Seeds – sebaceous cysts. Roots – deeper conditions.

Cornsilk (*Zea mays*) – for inflamed urinary passages, prostate, reproductive gland secretions. Combine with juniper berries and boneset.

Damiana – (*Turnera aphrodisiaca*) – general stimulant and sexual tonic. Aphrodisiac – make as tea, wine, burn as incense, smoke. Works well with saw palmetto – builds strength and flesh.

Saw palmetto (*Serenoa repens, S. serrulata*) – nutritive, diuretic, urinary antiseptic, endocrine agent. Enhances male sex hormones. Increases bladder tone, allows better contraction. 25–30 drops tincture 3 times a day.

Thyme – antiseptic, used for 'overly active' people.

Yarrow (*Achillea millefolium*) – general tonic – diaphoretic, hypotensive, astringent, diuretic, antiseptic, alterative.

Juniper – antiseptic tonic for the urinary tract, bladder and prostate.

Zinc – important for sexual development. Essential for production of testosterone. Even slight deficiency can lead to sexual dysfunction, impotence, lack of sexual vigour. Alcohol and drugs require greater demand. Occurs naturally in fish, meat, eggs. Chickweed, nettles, tuna. Aids energy metabolism. Zinc helps you think! Prevents body odour – deodorises the sweat glands. Prostate health – 100 mg a day.

Hormonal precursor foods – garlic, onions, peas, potatoes. Shown to ease PMS in women and low libido in men.

COMMON IMBALANCES

Cryptorchism – non-descent of testicles heats up abdominal cavity – can deteriorate and become cancerous. Begin treatment at age 5. Oriental treatment – acupuncture. AMA – drugs, surgery.

Holistic – tincture of

> Saw palmetto 1
> Blackberry
> Nettles 2
> Alfalfa 2

Parsley 2
Motherwort 1

20 drops 3 times a day until testicles descend.

Should stimulate testicle to descend either temporarily or permanently. Opt for surgery after 1 year.

Epididymitis – inflammation of the epididymis. Tincture of yarrow, thyme, saw palmetto, burdock and cleavers.

Sitz bath

$\frac{1}{2}$ cup bentonite clay.
1 quart comfrey, marjoram and sage tea.
10 drops lavender and 5 drops sage essential oil.
Enough tepid water to fill tub half-way.

Do twice daily.

Impotence

Diet – alkaline – 70% vegetables, fruit, potatoes.
Initiate lifestyle moderation – too much, too often.
Delete coffee, nicotine, drugs, alcohol.
100 mg. zinc a day.

Tincture of

Damiana – 1 oz.
Wild oats – 1 oz.
Saw palmetto – 1 oz.
Borage – 2 oz.
Nettles – 2 oz.
Yarrow –1 oz.

1 tsp. 4 times a day.

Orchitis

Infection of the testes, usually a virus, treat like epididymitis.
1 gram of Vitamin C daily.

Prostate health

Sunflower seeds
Zinc and Vitamin C
Low-fat diet

Herbs for bladder=herbs for prostate
Boneset
Dandelion
Burdock root
Juniper
Saw palmetto

Scrotal eczema

Calendula/comfrey infused oil with tea tree essential oil applied topically.
Burdock root tea, 3 cups a day.

Spermatorrhoea

Excessive emission of sperm without orgasm.

Tea of equal parts

Yarrow
Raspberry or blackberry
Sage

Drink two cups a day.

Venereal diseases

Antibiotics first, then detoxify with herbs.
Cleavers
Dock
Dandelion
Thyme

Venereal warts and herpes

Viral infections.
Zinc and Vitamin C
Anti-virals
Mugwort/marshmallow root tea topically – two times a day
Tea tree or thuja essential oil – 'paint' onto the warts or sores
Nervines

Herbal aphrodisiacs

Saw palmetto
Damiana

Yohimbe – don't take with alcohol, meat, or cheese
Coriander
Cardamom
Jasmine
Orange buds
Wild oats
Yarrow

SACRED HERBS FOR MEN

Green Man oil/incense

Juniper
Pine
Cedarwood
Oakmoss

Dagda incense

Oak leaves
Heather
Apple blossoms
Blackberry leaves
Daisy

Lugh incense

Frankincense
Calendula flowers
Vervain
Yarrow blossoms

THE CARDIO-VASCULAR/CIRCULATORY SYSTEM

Your heart never rests. It started to beat before you were born and will go on beating throughout your life.

The heart is made of cardiac muscle, which is as strong as a football. It gets bigger as you grow. It's about the size of your clenched fist and weighs about 11 oz.

Surrounded by your lungs and protected by your ribs, your heart works like a powerful pump, sending blood, with its cargo of oxygen and nutrients, to every part of your body.

Your heart changes speed, beating faster or slower, depending on how much your body needs.

Inside your heart

The heart is divided vertically into two halves, lying to the right and left of each other, separated by a septum.

Each half is divided horizontally into two chambers. The upper chamber of each half is called the atrium. The bottom chamber is called the ventricle.

The atriums fill with blood at the same time. Their thin, muscular walls squeeze blood into the ventricles via valves (one-way doors) that close firmly once the blood has passed through.

The valves

The valves between the atriums and the ventricles make sure that blood always flows in the same direction.

The tricuspid valve separates the right atrium and the right ventricle.

The mitral valve separates the left atrium and the left ventricle.

These valves open to allow blood to pass from the atrium to the ventricle then close to stop the blood from flowing backwards. Each time the valves close, they make the 'lub' sound of the heartbeat.

Blood leaves the heart through a second set of valves called the semilunar valves. When these close, they make the 'dub' sound of the heartbeat.

When the ventricles have filled with blood, they then squeeze and push blood into the arteries.

The right side of your heart receives all the deoxygenated blood from the rest of your body and sends it back to your lungs to receive new oxygen.

This 'fresh' blood then flows back to the left side of your heart to begin a new journey around your body. The left ventricle has to pump blood all around your body. To give it extra strength, its muscular walls are thicker than those of the right ventricle.

A circular system

Your heart is at the centre of the transport system of your body. Circulation is the continual circuit of the arteries carrying blood to every part of your body and the veins bringing it back to the heart.

There are three main parts. One circuit connects the heart to the lungs, from the right ventricle to the left atrium. The second circuit collects blood from the abdomen and carries it to the liver. The third circuit sends blood around the rest of your body and back again.

Pulmonary circulation

This is the journey of blood through the heart to the lungs and back again. Blood carrying carbon dioxide collects in the right atrium, then flows through the tricuspid valve to the right ventricle.

It is then pumped to the lungs. In the alveoli of the lungs, the carbon dioxide is exchanged for oxygen.

The oxygenated blood then flows back through pulmonary veins to the left atrium, through the mitral valve to the left ventricle. It leaves the heart through the semi-lunar valve.

Blood is pumped to the rest of the body, delivering oxygen and nutrients where needed and picking up carbon dioxide.

It returns through the veins to the right atrium to begin again.

The journey of blood through the heart

Deoxygenated blood from the rest of the body comes into the right atrium through the tricuspid valve to the right ventricle; through the semi-lunar valve to the lungs, where oxygen is picked up; to the left atrium through the mitral valve; to the left ventricle through the semi-lunar valve; to the body.

What is blood for?

Your blood acts like a delivery service, carrying oxygen, nutrients and antibodies to all parts of your body. Hormones, vitamins, salts and minerals are taken where needed and where they will be most useful.

It then picks up carbon dioxide and waste products and carries them away to be filtered and removed from the body. The carbon dioxide is taken to the lungs to be breathed out and the wastes are sent to the liver and kidneys to be excreted.

The water in blood plasma bathes your cells and keeps everything lubricated.

Blood contains special chemicals, which form clots, sealing off cuts in your skin.

White blood cells fight infection from harmful bacteria and viruses.

Blood helps to control body temperature by absorbing heat from busy organs such as the liver and heart, taking it to cooler resting places so that heat is spread more evenly.

Blood makes a complete circuit around the body in about 1 minute at rest and about every 20 seconds during strenuous exercise.

Your hardworking heart

At rest, the average adult heart beats 60–80 times a minute, and the average child's heart beats 120 times a minute. Just to give some perspective, the average elephant's heart beats 25 times a minute.

The adult human heart beats 100,000 times a day, 40 million times a year! As blood leaves the heart, it travels at a speed at 30 cm. per second. 5 to 7 litres of blood are pumped through the body every minute.

What is blood made of?

More than 50% of blood volume is made up of a yellowish fluid called plasma which is made up of 90% water and 10% digested foods, minerals, salts and hormones, fats, sugars and proteins.

45% is made up of blood cells or corpuscles. There are three kinds of blood cells.
1. Red blood cells or erythrocytes have a large surface area to hold oxygen and are very flexible to be able to squeeze through capillaries. They take their colour from haemoglobin, made from protein and iron. They are like mothers, continually feeding and cleaning up!
2. White blood cells or leucocytes are the warriors. They protect your body from viruses and bacteria.
3. Platelets are cell fragments that help blood to clot.

The average human body has about 9 pints (5 litres) of blood.

Herbs for the blood

Burdock – has long been reputed as an anti-cancer, anti-tumour herb. It has been shown to bind to and remove heavy metals and chemicals from the blood.

Cleavers – dissolves blood clots and strengthens veins. Used to prevent stroke.

Dandelion – aids liver and urinary system to filter wastes from the blood.

Nettles – high in iron, nettles helps build blood and improves clotting.

Plantain – high in iron.

Red clover – alkalinises and builds blood. Latest tests in Germany are showing an ability to turn off oncogenes (cancer cells), reduce tumours and growths and repair damaged DNA.

Vascular tonics – strengthen the vessels. Hawthorn, calendula, St. John's wort, yarrow.

Urinary tonics – kidneys filter the blood and create blood pressure. Take good care of them! Dandelion, burdock, cleavers, yarrow.

Vulneraries – repair damaged vessels. Calendula, comfrey, plantain, St. John's wort.

Bitters – aid the liver. Dandelion, dock, yarrow, etc.

Demulcents – aid hydration. Mallow, marshmallow, plantain.

Lymphatics – aid filtering. Burdock, cleavers, calendula.

Circulatory foods – these help keep the vessels clear and promote elasticity. Oats, beets, artichokes, green leaf vegetables, raw garlic, onions, warm lemon water, apple cider vinegar.

BLOOD VESSEL IMBALANCES

Varicosities – varicose veins and haemorrhoids

Varicosities are enlarged, twisted, swollen veins that can occur anywhere in the body, usually the legs. When they occur on the anus, they are called haemorrhoids.

They can be symptom-free or aching, heavy and painful. Women are four times more likely to have them as men. In the US, the most common causes are sedentary life-style and lack of fibre in the diet.

Deep varicosities can lead to pulmonary embolism, myocardial infarction and stroke. While herbal care can certainly help, laser therapy may want to be considered in serious cases. Prevention is the best course.

Varicosities occur due to weak venous system valves. Upon standing, venous pressure becomes very high. Fluid leaks from capillary blood into the tissues, causing oedema. This prevents diffusion of nutritional substances from the blood to muscles and skin, causing pain and weakness.

Preventing and eliminating varicose veins and haemorrhoids

Internally

A possible formula is as follows. Equal parts of

Yarrow – alterative, astringent, bitter, vascular tonic, urinary tonic.

Cleavers – astringent, strengthens veins, prevents clots, lymphatic and urinary tonic.

Plantain – a vulnerary and a demulcent to balance the necessary astringency of the yarrow and cleavers.

Make the above as a vodka or apple cider vinegar tincture and take 1 tsp. three times a day.

Also apply daily as a liniment to the site of the varicosity and massage upward toward the heart. Add lavender essential oil for itching and inflammation.

Do NOT apply this topically to haemorrhoids, as it will sting badly! Instead, apply yarrow tea with lavender essential oil after each bowel movement.

The application of rose water will reduce swelling and pain of both varicosities and haemorrhoids.

Migraines

Inflamed arteries constrict and then dilate intensely, causing severe throbbing, always beginning and often remaining on one side of the head. They are accompanied by nausea, with or without vomiting.

There are sometimes warning symptoms before the onset of pain called auras. Typical auras last a few minutes and include visual blurring or bright spots, anxiety, fatigue, disturbed thinking, numbness or tingling on one side of the body.

The attack typically starts in the morning, peaks within an hour, lasts 4–24 hours and can occur several times a month. Contributing factors include:

> Vascular instability
> Bowel toxaemia
> Hormonal imbalance
> Emotional changes such as post-stress letdown, anger
> Exhaustion

Feverfew is the most excellent and effective herb for migraines. As a bitter, it detoxifies the bowels and aids hormonal balance. It is used fresh, as a tincture, or eating the fresh leaf.

1 tsp. of tincture or 1 fresh leaf a day as a tonic preventive.

1 tsp. of tincture at the onset of the aura, then follow with 1 tsp. every 6 hours for 24 hours.

Also incorporate the following:

> Yarrow – vascular tonic, bitter
> Crampbark – anti-spasmodic
> Cleavers or red clover – natural blood thinners

WEAVING THE WEB

Suggestions for working with the lessons of this chapter

Write your own 'Making Poem'. Create some of the blessings to empower the sacred masculine.

Contemplate your own relationship to the masculine.

Study the chapter on the cardio-vascular system. Could your heart, or someone's you know, use some nurturing?

Obtain and work with three **Materia Medica** *herbs. Record your experiences.*

Blessings of the Dagda the Good Father,
Lugh the Many-skilled One
and Angus, God of Love, upon you!

CHAPTER 9

MATERIA MEDICA

BLACKBERRY

(*Rubus fructicosus*). Irish – Muin Dubh. Perennial.
Folk names: Blackbrides, bramble, goutberry, Doctor's medicine, etc.
Family: Rosacea.
Habitat: Waste places, edges of woods, full sun. Native to Europe.
Parts used: Leaves, roots, flowers and berries.
Leaves: Cut stems with new, young leaves in the spring. Remove the
   leaves from the stems and lay on flat trays.
Flowers: Gather gently in the summer and lay face down on linen or
   muslin to dry.
Fruit and root: Pluck the berries into buckets in the autumn, trying not to
   eat them all! Dig the root after the first good rain has softened the
   Earth.
Constituents: Tannins, Vitamin C, calcium, trace minerals, flavanoids.
Actions: Nutritive, tonic, astringent, diuretic.

Specific uses
- Leaf is an excellent daily nutritive tonic.
- Diarrhoea, haemorrhoids – the root is the strongest.
- Cystitis.
- Mouthwash, gargle – sore throat, sore gums, laryngitis.
- Reproductive and fertility tonic – safe for pregnancy – strengthens the
  womb.
- Tones and strengthens muscular and organ tissues.
- General daily tonic: 3 cups a day for an adult.

Metaphysical

Plant of Fire and Earth

Blackberry is one of Brighid's favoured healing plants. Blackberry strengthens the physical body and is a warrior for Mother Earth. Just as blackberry grows to protect Her where the ground has been disturbed and made vulnerable, so will she offer us the same protection. She provides sanctuary for small animals and Nature Spirits. Blackberry bestows the blessings of strength, determination, prosperity and protection and helps in creating and maintaining healthy boundaries. Blackberry has taught me to 'claim my space' and showed me how sometimes we intrude on others' space. That's when she creeps in the garden and I have to 'help her contain herself' and not crowd out the other plants. I see this as very much like the mother who has to answer the cry 'Mom! They're in my room, again!' and teach the invading sibling about personal boundaries. Anything that blackberry extends beyond her established boundaries is her offering of nourishment and medicine. Dry and/or tincture the leaves and flowers, eat the berries, make wine or syrups from them, dig the roots up where she shouldn't grow and dry and/or tincture.

BORAGE

(*Boragio off.*). Irish – an Borrach.
Family: Boraginaceae.
Parts used: Leaves and flowers.
Habitat: Full sun, near dwellings. Native to Europe.
Constituents: Saponins, mucilage, tannins, essential oil, allantoin, silicic acid, Vitamin C, calcium, potassium.
Seeds: essential fatty acids including *cis*-linoleic and gamma-linoleic acids.
Actions: Leaves/flowers – adrenal/nervine tonic, adaptogen, galactogogue, diuretic, febrifuge, anti-rheumatic, diaphoretic, expectorant, demuculent, anti-depressant (depression, grief and anxiety). Seeds (oil) – relieves eczema, anti-rheumatic, anti-inflammatory (irritable bowel, colitis), menstrual regulator.

Specific uses

- Tonifies the adrenal cortex, increasing the ability to cope during stress.
- Aids the adrenal production of oestrogen/progesterone during menopause.
- Healing for fevers, helpful in convalescence.

• Post-partum de-stresser, promotes milk flow.

Applications: Infusion, fresh or dry, 1 cup 3 times a day. Tincture, 20 drops 3 times a day. Lotion. Flower syrup, 1 tsp. 3 times a day.

Metaphysical

Plant of Fire and the Warrior.

Known as 'Herb of Gladness', the name is derived from the Gaelic word 'Borrach', meaning courage. Borage strengthens the heart and the will and bestows courage when facing conflict. Borage is the plant that Celtic warriors ingested prior to battle. It was given to games participants at Lughnassagh and served at festivals to make men and women merry and ensure hearts of gladness.

Borage fortifies the inner self and helps us to face the challenge bravely and graciously and to adapt to change. It aids psychic powers and offers strength, courage and endurance for vision quests, inner journeys and initiations. To invoke these gifts, use as a flower essence, ritual tea and/ or bath herb.

BURDOCK

(*Arctium lappa*). Irish – an Cnadan Mor.
Folk names: Cockle buttons, beggar's buttons, love leaves, happy major, thorny burr, clot burr, fox clote.
Family: Compositae.
Habitat: Waste grounds, roadsides, by old buildings. Burdock is a biennial, liking the damp and part-shade to sun.
Parts used: The root, gathered in the first year of growth. It deteriorates the second year when the plant sets seed and dies back. The leaf, gathered almost any time, if structurally sound. Take one or two from each plant. Some herbalists use the seed, but I find them too painful to work with. Better to leave them to propagate new plants!
Constituents: Root: bitter principle, inulin, mucilage, fixed and volatile oils, resin, crystalline glycoside, starch.
Actions: Root: alterative, anti-scorbutic, diuretic, diaphoretic, astringent, demulcent (therefore amphoteric) stomachic, liver and kidney tonic, vulnerary. Tests have shown that burdock binds to heavy metals and chemicals and removes them from the blood.
Leaves: Anti-inflammatory, vulnerary.

Specific uses

Root:

- Blood disorders, including arthritis, rheumatism, gout and anaemia. Latest studies show that burdock binds and removes heavy metals and chemicals from the body and is gaining reputation as an anti-cancer/anti-tumour herb.
- Skin diseases – eczema, acne, psoriasis, boils, scurvy.
- Shingles – combine with St. John's wort.
- Post-drug blood purifier and de-toxifier.
- Kidney diseases.
- Prostate and other male reproductive issues.
- Cancer and AIDS.
- The leaf is used as a poultice for sprains, swellings, burns, bruises, and other inflammations. Pound the leaves into a mash and apply to the affected area.

Applications

- Fresh root tincture – standard jar method.
- Dry root tincture – standard jar method.
- Both make a lovely, milky rich tincture.
- Tea – fresh or dry root – 1–2 cups a day.

IMPORTANT! Burdock is a very strong blood purifier, causing toxins to be released quickly into the bloodstream. This can precipitate the experience of 'getting worse before getting better', even causing blood poisoning. Make sure the organs of elimination are in good condition to deal with the wastes as they are released. Offer no more than 2 cups of tea or 2 droppers of tincture a day.

A traditional method of preparation

Take 1 oz. of root and $1\frac{1}{2}$ pints of cold water and steep for 3 hours, then decoct for 20 minutes. Drink 1–2 wineglassfuls a day.

Metaphysics

Herb of Water

Burdock offers purification, pulling things up from deep down so that they may be released, restoring strength and virility.

Incorporate the leaves into incenses and baths.

The roots can be cut into small pieces and strung onto red thread as a protective amulet.

Burdock ensures survivability.

CALENDULA

(*Calendula off.*). Irish – or Mhiré.
Folk name: Pot marigold.
Family: *Compositae*.
Habitat: Full sun, native of Europe.
Parts used: Flowers.
Constituents: Saponins, flavanoids, mucilage, essential oil, bitter principle, resin, steroidal compounds.
Actions: Astringent, antiseptic, anti-fungal, anti-microbial, anti-inflammatory, bitter tonic, vulnerary, menstrual regulator, stimulates, bile production, lymphatic, antispasmodic.

Specific uses

- Skin inflammations – sore nipples, scalds, sunburn, eczema.
- Gynaecological issues.
- Toxic conditions.
- Yeast infections.
- Inflammation of the oesophagus.
- Sluggish digestion.
- Varicose ulcers, slow healing wounds.
- Mouth ulcers and gum disease.
- Anxiety and depression.

Applications

- Tea, three cups a day.
- Tincture, three tsp. a day.
- Oil, cream, salve, steams and washes.

Metaphysics

Herb of the Sun, Herb of Fire

Calendula helps us to embrace our success and enhances confidence.
A herb of consecration for rites of passage.
In funereal blends, it blesses the departed soul.
Use dry petals as incense or macerate in sunflower oil for an anointing oil.

CHAMOMILE

Roman or common (*Anthemis nobilis*). German (Matricaria chamomilla).
Irish – an Mhea Drua.
Family: *Compositae*.
Folknames: Ground apples (the scent is similar to apples), pinheads.
Habitat: NW and SW Europe – Spain, France, England, Ireland,
Germany, Greece, spread to and naturalised in Asia and North Africa.

Since the most ancient times, perhaps no herb has been so widely used
by the common folk of Europe as chamomile. The Greeks named it
kamai (ground) melon (apple) and the Spaniards called it manzanilla
(little apple). They introduced the double-flowered variety to Germany
at the close of the Middle Ages and Germany is now the largest consumer
and cultivator.

Chamomile can grow in poor soil, likes full Sun, requires water and
loves to be walked on, which stimulates growth. Called 'the gardener's
physician', she heals and strengthens the other plants she grows around.
Plant chamomile around a sickly plant and it will usually recover!
Parts used: Flowers. Double head varieties are resistant to frost.
Constituents: Both species are medicinal – the 'apple smell' will be
evidence of the medicine. Volatile oils, azulene, flavanoids, bitter principle, coumarins (anti-spasmodic, anti-thrombotic), tannins, mucilage,
magnesium, niacin, phosphorus, choline.
Actions: Mild bitter, anti-inflammatory, anti-spasmodic, nervous, digestive, urinary and circulatory tonic, relaxant (providing calm in the
midst of chaos), antiseptic, anti-microbial, anti-bacterial, anti-fungal,
carminative, diaphoretic, diuretic, decongestant, vulnerary.

Specific uses

A wonderful all-round, multi-faceted plant, chamomile helps to heal the
following.

- Digestive disorders – speeding recovery and preventing ulcers, gas,
  colic, gastritis, colitis, diarrhoea and constipation (helps to regulate
  peristalsis). Cleansing to the liver and gall bladder, stimulating digestion.
- Skin ulcers and inflammations, burns and wounds. Sore, red eyes.
- Varicose veins and haemorrhoids. Add to baths, creams, salves and
  massage oils for sore nipples, eczema, rashes, muscular aches and pains.

Use internally and externally for the following.

- Urinary infections – the antiseptic oils help soothe bladder inflammations and cystitis and gently de-toxify the kidneys.
- Gynaecological issues – painful menses, PMS headaches, including migraines, absence of bleeding due to stress (combine with lemon balm). As a douche for vaginal infections.
- Respiratory allergies and infections – anti-inflammatory and decongestant.
- Aches and pains of all kinds – head, nerve, flu, arthritic and rheumatic.

Applications

- Tea – 1 tsp. herb to 1 cup water, infused, up to 4 times a day; or tincture – 1 tsp. 3 times a day.
- Steam inhalations – for asthma, allergies, sinusitis, skin inflammations.
- Cosmetics, massage oils, baths.
- Douche – make a strong tea and apply 2 times a day for three days.
- Child and Elder safe.

Metaphysical

Herb of Air and gentle Herb of Fire.

- Soothes and blesses the inner child.
- Blesses new beginnings.
- Empowers the solar plexus.
- Honours and invokes Sun deities.
- Draws prosperity.
- A guardian in the garden.
- Transforms negative energy.

Add to incense and ceremonial tea blends; add to anointing oils by infusing the fresh or dry flowers in carrier oil or add drops of the essential oil. Chamomile is wonderful in the bath and dream pillows.

CHICKWEED

(*Stellaria media*). Irish – an fliodh.
Folknames: Starweed, satinflower, adder's mouth, stitchwort, cluckenwort, starwort.
Family: Carophyllaceae.
Habitat: Eurasia. Wasteplaces, roadsides, gardens, cultivated land, rich, moist soil, open cool environs – helps soil retain nitrogen, indicates fertile, mineral rich soil.

Parts used: aerial.
Constituents: steroidal saponins, minerals, Vitamins A, B and C, mucilage, silica, fatty acids.
Actions: Nutritive tonic, cell permeator, astringent, demulcent, emollient, anti-rheumatic, refrigerant, vulnerary, expectorant, lymphatic and endo-crine tonic, diuretic, anti-inflammatory, anti-pyretic, alterative, pectoral, dissolves growths, laxative, diuretic, high in Vitamins A, B and C and minerals – calcium, potassium.

Specific uses
- Urinary tract inflammations – cystitis.
- Lung treatments – dissolves thickened lung and throat membranes.
- Increases absorption of nutrients from the digestive mucosa.
- Neutralises toxins.
- Dissolves warts and cysts (especially ovarian).
- Respiratory inflammation.
- Alleviates itching and inflammation.
- Eczema, psoriasis, hives, surface veins – apply as poultice.
- Rheumatic inflammation – breaks down uric acid.
- Draws out splinters, heals wounds.
- Tonic – constipation, cystitis, general weakness.

Metaphysical

Herb of Air

Increases permeability to cosmic energies.

- Strengthens the crown chakra.
- Bestows the energy of the stars.
- Helps us to release old patterns and begin new ones.
- Blessings of and for the child.
- Renewal.

Applications
- Use fresh as tea or tincture – 1 tsp. 3–6 times a day.
- Chickweed is one of the spring tonic vinegar herbs.
- Salve or compress, combined with mallow, ground ivy and chamomile. Use as needed for swellings and skin inflammations.

Chickweed is a spring 'grazing' herb – eat it fresh in salads, it will help release the winter and prepare the body and psyche for spring.

CLEAVERS

(*Gallium aparine*, *Gallium* spp.). Irish – an Garbhlus. A native British herb.
Family: *Rubinaceae* (madder family).
Folknames: Goose grass, Our Lady's Bedstraw, gravel grass, maids hair.
Habitat: moist meadows and woods, seashores, stony alpine slopes.
Parts used: Spring/summer – aerial parts. Summer/autumn – seeds (coffee substitute). Autumn/spring – roots (for dye).
Constituents: Glycoside asperuloside, tannins, gallotannic acid, citric acid, coumarin.
Actions: Lymphatic, anti-lithic, anti-tumour, refrigerant, diuretic, hepatic, alterative, anti-inflammatory, astringent.

Specific uses
- Regulates fluid balance and body weight.
- Cysts, cystitis, painful urination, gravel in urinary tract.
- Lymphatic cancer, tumours.
- Mouth cancer, goitre.
- Releases toxic wastes from organs.
- Psoriasis and ulcerous skin inflammations.
- Aches, pains and sore muscles.
- Lymphodenitis (swollen glands); stimulates lymphatic drainage.
- Tonsillitis and adenoid trouble.

Applications

For medicinal purposes, cleavers needs to be fresh.

- 1 tablespoon to 1 cup boiling water, 3 times a day.
- Tincture – apple cider vinegar or alcohol, 3 tsp. a day.
- External wash/poultice, 3 times a day.
- Gargle (short term – long use can cause mouth inflammations), 2 times a day. Combine with demulcents, e.g. mallow, comfrey.

Metaphysics

Herb of Air, herb of Renewal

Like Spider Grandmother, cleavers filters out that which we no longer need, draws to us that which we do need and re-weaves our Web of Being.

Cleavers will help to draw and bind to us the qualities we are seeking while filtering out the obstacles we may be creating.

Use the fresh herb tea or tincture as part of the ritual drink or in the bath or the dried herb in an incense.

Like a fresh breeze, cleavers moves stagnant water.

An olde recipe for spring renewal

Take the fresh herb, pound well, then put in an unglazed earthenware vessel and fill lightly, cover with pure spring water and let stand overnight. Strain and drink.

Cleavers drawing ball

Write out your desire on some special paper, fold into a small packet and wrap a bunch of seeding cleavers around it to make a ball. Place on your altar and 'feed' it with ritual until it dries. Then bury it in the Earth during an Earth or Water Moon. Water well. By the time the new cleavers grows in, your wish will have been made manifest.

COMFREY

(*Symphytum off.*). Irish – an Compar.
Folknames: Boneset, knitbone, woundwort, healall, stitchwort.
Family: Boraginaceae.
Habitat: Europe and Siberia.
Parts used: Leaf and root – dry.
Constituents: Allantoin, tannins, mucilage; saponins, alkaloids (absent in dried leaf) protein (more than soy), iron, potassium, calcium, Vitamins A, B12, C, D and E, inulin, magnesium, zinc, 18 amino acids.
Actions: Demuculent, vulnerary, mild astringent, expectorant, nutrient.

Comfrey has had such bad press, but I love this plant! Comfrey offers herself as a vegetable, tea, healing herb, compost activator, garden fertiliser (just lay the leaves around your plants), and livestock food. Comfrey controls cell formation and reduces abnormal growths.

The alkaloids of so much concern disappear in the leaves when they are dry. If you still are concerned, don't use the plant internally, but use it as an external remedy and as food for your garden – there is no finer fertiliser!

Specific uses

- Intestinal disorders and inflammation.
- Diarrhoea and dysentery.

- Lung disorders, coughs, bronchitis.
- Internal haemorrhage.
- Sprains, swelling, bruises, broken bones.
- Stomach and duodenal ulcers.
- Diverticulitis.
- Varicose ulcers.

Applications

- Tea, tincture – dried herb 3 times a day.
- Fresh leaf poultice, oil or salve for external bites, rashes, cuts, bruises, arthritis – not deep wounds.
- Gastric inflammation – combines well with mallow, meadowsweet, mint, chamomile.
- Bronchial – with coltsfoot, horehound, elecampane.
- Wounds – with calendula.

Metaphysics

Herb of Earth and Saturn

A plant of abundance and prosperity, comfrey offers many gifts, including the following.
- Grounding.
- Connections and rootedness.
- Strength and stamina.
- Aid with physical manifestation.
- Comfort.
- Nurturing.
- Structure.
- Safety while travelling – place in shoes, suitcase, car to prevent loss and accident.

DANDELION

(*Taraxacum off.*). Irish: an Caiserarbhan.
Folknames: Dent de lion (the leaves look like lions' teeth), piss en lit (piss-in-the-bed – it's a diuretic), wild endive, cankerwort.
Family: *Compositae*.
Habitat: Native of Eurasia, now naturalised everywhere. Pastures, meadows, waste ground, sidewalks.

Parts used: Leaves and flowers in spring and summer. The young leaves are great in salads. The older the leaves, the higher the bitter principle – too bitter for most folk to eat, but potent medicine.

Gather roots in the autumn for inulin, in spring for taraxacum, taraxacin. Actually, dandelion can be gathered all year round. It is supportive and nutrient at any time. I gather leaf and root in the spring, the whole plant including the flower in summer, the root and leaf in the autumn. When preparing whole plant, cut the leaves and roots from the crown. Compost the crown. Separate the flowers from the stems and compost the stems. Chop up the leaves and roots and add them to the flowers in a jar to make tincture.

Constituents: Inulin (root and flower), bitter principle, glycosides, potassium, tannins, Vitamins C and B2 (leaves and flowers), latex, taraxacum, taraxacin, Vitamins A and E, iron, phosphorus, ascorbic acid, zinc and other trace minerals, saponins, phytosterols, essential fatty acids.

Actions

Tonic for

- Liver (root).
- Kidneys (leaves).
- Pancreas (flowers).
- Endocrine/hormonal balancer.

Diuretic, laxative, cholagogue, adaptogen, alterative.

Specific uses

- Kidney diseases – prevents/eliminates gallstones and kidney stones.
- Eliminates excess fluids and toxins, while contributing potassium (unlike pharmaceutical diuretics which deplete potassium).
- Oedema, gout.
- Cystitis – combine with an anti-microbial.
- Digestive/bowel disorders – hepatitis, anaemia, jaundice, cirrhosis, colitis.
- Rheumatic – breaks down uric acid in cartilage and tendons.
- Promotes digestion, stimulates appetite for better assimilation.
- Lowers cholesterol and balances blood pressure.
- Skin disorders – scurvy, eczema, acne.
- Thyroid disorders.
- Hormonal imbalances.

Applications

I like to use the whole plant as much as possible.

Tea: root (dry or fresh) decoction and/or leaf and flower infusion: 3 cups a day.

Tincture: whole plant – 20 drops, 3 times a day.

Dandelion absorbs through the skin via steams, baths and lotions.

Dandelion flower oil is wonderful for glowing skin and supple muscles.

Metaphysical

Plant of Fire and the Sun

Another of Brighid's favourite plants, considered by the Celts to be sacred to Herself and to Lugh, the Sun-God, and Graine, the Sun-Goddess, dandelion is my personal totem ally and the plant I love the most.

Purposely imported to America by the *Mayflower* voyagers, dandelion is one of our best healing and nutritive allies.

Dandelion will not be vanquished (even though billions of dollars are spent every year trying!), literally growing through concrete to express itself, adapting to whatever conditions it finds itself in, bestowing the same strength, determination and adaptability upon us. Use the tea or infused oil in rituals.

Dandelion empowers the solar plexus, the will 'to be' and confident self-expression. She teaches the balance of true humbleness and true confidence. Dry and place some root and/or leaf in amulet bags or add the fresh flower tea to your bath to strengthen these powers. Grow at the NW corner of the house for favourable winds.

Dandelion is one of the 'weeds' that actually helps to heal the soil by transporting minerals up through the layers. It adapts itself to grow lower than the mower blade (and some people will insist that plants don't have a consciousness!).

It is so ironic that the eradication of the dandelion is a billion-dollar business in this country! So, encourage your friends to not spray the dandelions, but to let them grow for their beauty and their medicine.

An olde recipe

'Take dandelion, corn blue bottle and garden parsley, pound them well with a good strong ale, and keep it carefully in a narrow mouthed water bottle. Let it be used the first thing in the morning an hour before food, and the last thing at night after food. The dose should be from four eggshellfuls to a pint'.

191

DOCK

(*Rumex crispus*/*R. oblusifolius*) Perennial. Irish – an Chopog Chatach (meaning curly auricle of light).
Folknames: Bloodwort, yellow dock.
Family: *Polygonaceae*.
Parts used: Root gathered in autumn.
Habitat: Native to Europe – roadsides, wasteground, gardens and meadows.
Constituents: Tannins, volatile oil, oxalates (higher in leaves). Anthraqui-none glycosides (laxative) (including nepodin, emodin, chrysapharol), Vitamin C, iron, Vitamin A, manganese.
Actions: Bitter, alterative, laxative, cleansing, de-toxifying, chologogue.

Specific uses

- Constipation, sluggish digestion.
- Blood disorders (anaemia).
- Rheumatism and arthritis.
- Skin diseases – boils, stings, eczema, psoriasis, fungal infections, acne, etc.
- Tuberculosis.
- Syphilis.
- De-toxifying – it has been claimed that dock arrests the onset of cancer.

Applications

- Decoction – 1 cup 3 times a day – 1 week on, 1 week off.
- Tincture – 1 dropper 3 times a day – 1 week on, 1 week off.
- Salve – itchy skin, bites, bruises.
- Leaf poultice – stings, warts, bruised skin or facial steam for skin eruptions.

Metaphysical

Plant of Fire, Summer Solstice, the Warrior

- Imparts courage and strength and facilitates development of magical will.
- Attracts money – infusion of the root sliced in medallions (they look like gold coins), sprinkled around the business, will attract customers.
- Fertility – the woman wishing to conceive ties a little bag of the seeds to her left arm.

- Use as a tea for releasing anger. (Create ritual space and choose a physical method to facilitate physical expression of that anger, e.g. breaking dishes, tearing up phonebooks, etc. Burn vervain afterwards and drink vervain tea to restore peace to yourself and the space.

ELDER

(*Sambuccus nigra*). Irish – an Ruis an Trom.
Family: *Caprifoliaceae*.
Folknames: The Old Mother, Lady Ellhorn, Elder Mother, Queen of the Elves, black elder, pipe tree, bour tree, witch tree.
Habitat: Native to Europe and western Asia. Thirty species worldwide, widely cultivated. Elder likes waterside thickets and hedgerows.
Parts used: Flowers, berries (blue only – red ones are toxic). Harvest from *Sambuccus nigra* only. Bark and leaves are used externally only. Taken internally, they are purgative.
Constituents: Flowers: flavanoids, tannins, volatile oil, mucilage. Berries: flavanoids, tannins, viburnic acid (induces perspiration), sugars, pectin, Vitamins A, B and C, organic acids.
Actions: Flowers: alterative, anti-inflammatory, antiseptic, vulnerary, gently expectorant, mild laxative, diuretic, diaphoretic, febrifuge, cosmetic, pulmonary tonic, anti-catarrhal, emollient, demulcent. Berries: alterative, diuretic, laxative, diaphoretic, demulcent, pulmonary tonic, anti-spasmodic, calming.

Specific uses

Flowers:

- Upper and lower respiratory infections; colds and flus with chills – take as a hot tea.
- Febrifuge – elder works harmoniously with yarrow to manage fevers, induce perspiration and shorten a flu to half its time.
- Gargle with the tea for hoarseness, laryngitis and gum inflammations.
- Skin inflammations: use the tea as a cosmetic and anti-inflammatory healer in compresses, creams and lotions for burns, rashes and growths.

Berries:

- Respiratory infections, colds and flus.
- Stubborn coughs.
- Nerve inflammations – neuralgia, sciatica, migraine.
- Rheumatic pain.

- Eye complaints involving the nerves (internal application).

Applications

- Tea – flower infusion, berry decoction. 3 cups a day.
- Tincture – 3 teaspoons a day of berries. (No more! High doses are emetic!)
- Elderberry wine – infuse 2 handfuls of elder berries in $1\frac{1}{2}$ pints of red wine for two weeks. Strain and rebottle. Take heated for chills and flus.
- Elderberry cough syrup – tincture fresh elder berries in brandy or whiskey. Strain and add an equal amount of honey. Take by the teaspoonful up to 6 teaspoonfuls.
- Elderberry syrup – 1 cup elder berries, 2 cups water, 1 cup raw honey. Decoct elder berries in the water, allowing to simmer down to 1 cup of liquid. Mash berries well and then strain. Stir in the honey. Bottle. Take 1 tablespoon, 4 times a day, for colds and flus, etc.
- Fly-away flu tea – 1 oz. elder flowers, 1 oz. yarrow leaf and flower, $\frac{1}{2}$ oz. fennel. Mix together in a glass jar. Prepare an infusion of 1 tsp. per cup of boiling water. Take 4–6 cups a day. To induce a sweat, drink as hot as possible while wrapped in blankets. Allow perspiration for 30 minutes. Take a warm bath or shower, then go to bed for a refreshing sleep.
- Elderflower water – 5 cups of blossoms, $1\frac{1}{4}$ cups boiling water. Pour the water over the flowers, cover and let stand for 2–3 hours. Strain into a bottle and refrigerate. Apply daily with a cotton pad to soften, clear and lighten the complexion and to alleviate swollen, puffy eyes.
- Elderflower lotion – mix equal parts of the elderflower water and glycerine. Apply to the face and body to soften, smooth and beautify the skin.
- Fountain of youth tea – equal parts elderflowers, chamomile, and linden flowers. Infuse and drink two cups in the evening. Also relieves pain and inflammation.

Metaphysical aspects

The Moon, Neptune, The Crone

Elder is a tree of perfect balance and wholeness, her flowers representing the Bright Goddess, her berries, the Dark Goddess. The Elder Mother commands respect, good manners and honourable ethics in those who approach her. It is said she will follow and plague those who use her with selfish intent! Gypsies would never dream of burning the wood and hedgerow cutters would always separate the elder from the other trimmings to be burned.

The polite way to gather Mother Elder's gifts

This is an ancient tradition; variations of the words have been passed down for generations. It is an example of the respectful way to approach all plants and 'Elder Mothers' of all species, offering something of ourselves in exchange for their wisdom and healing.

Bow before the tree and say

Sacred Elder Mother,
If thou wilt give me some of thy wood,
I will give thee some of mine when I die.

Wait until she gives you permission by her silence and carefully gather some of her flowers or berries. *Never* take them all.

Leave a gift; a penny, some honey, a strand of your hair, for example.

The Celtic Druids gathered the last berries in December and made a ritual wine from them to aid clairvoyance and contact with the Tuatha de Danaan. Elder Mother is a gatekeeper between the realms. She serves as guide when we seek communion with our ancestors and various aspects of the divine. Elder will bring magic to the wish and intensify the power of any ritual she participates in. Make sure the working is honourable and ethical and be careful what you wish for! Add the flowers or berries to incenses or the ritual cup to invoke deep wisdom and magic.

The Elder Mother offers protection to farm and wild animals and expels negativity from the area where she grows. Twigs were carried to ward off rheumatism and tied into crosses with red yarn to guard homes and barns.

As a funereal herb, Mother Elder blesses the departed spirit with regeneration. The Celts planted it on new graves and, when it flowered, they knew the beloved had arrived and was happily settled in Tir-na-Nog, the Land of Youth.

Use the flowers in incenses, baths and infused wines to invoke the blessings of the Bright Mother.

Use the berries in incenses and infused wines to invoke the deep wisdom and primal power of the Dark Mother.

ELECAMPANE

(*Inula helenium*). Irish – Meacan Aillinn. Perennial.
Folknames: Wild sunflower, horseheal, velvet dock, scabwort, elfwort.

Family: *Compositae*.
Habitat: Part/full sun, deep loamy soil.
Parts used: Root (2nd year), leaves and flowers.
Constituents: Volatile oil (including helenium, azulene), inulin, sterols, resin, pectin, mucilage, bitter principle.
Actions: Bitter, anti-bacterial, anti-fungal, antiseptic, expectorant, anti-parasitic, diaphoretic, alterative, tonic, emmenagogue, diuretic, vulnerary, anti-catarrh, astringent, demuculent, anti-emetic.

Specifics: root

- Tonic – weakness following influenza, bronchitis, radiation, etc.
- Stubborn coughs and congestion – pulmonary infections.
- Blood sugar balance, anaemia.
- Upper respiratory, asthma, hay fever.
- Digestive and liver stimulant.
- Eczema, rashes, varicose ulcers.
- Intestinal parasites, pinworms, giardia (alantolactone).
- Nausea, vomiting.
- Flatulence, abdominal distension.
- Malnutrition, wasting diseases.
- Irregular cycles, post-partum restorative.

Dosage: Tea: dried root decoction – $\frac{1}{2}$ cup 2 times a day. Tincture: $\frac{1}{4}$–$\frac{1}{2}$ tsp. 3 times a day.

Metaphysics

Plant of Fire and the Sun

Elecampane dispels melancholy and causes mirth.

Elven magick – drink the leaf/flower infusion to help attune with them. Wear to draw love and protection.

A religious herb used by the Druids, tossed onto the fire to honour the Wildfolk.

FENNEL

(*Foeniculum vulgare*). Irish – an Finéal.
Habitat: Gardens, hedges meadows – originated in Mediterranean, India.
Parts used: whole plant, including root and seeds.
Constituents: Essential oil, flavanoids, coumarins.

Actions and uses: Expectorant, anti-inflammatory, carminative, antispasmodic, respiratory and digestive tonic. Discharges mucus from bronchial tubes, anti inflammatory. Disorders of the digestive tract. Carminative and antispasmodic. Eye inflammations, conjunctivitis, styes, etc.

Applications

- 1 tsp. crushed seed per cup boiling water 3 times a day.
- 2–3 tsp. tincture 3 times a day.
- Great synergiser for formulas.

Metaphysics

Plant of Air

- The herb of long life and vitality.
- Carry to have your words accepted with trust and without scepticism.
- Eat the seed to 'plant' new patterns of behaviour in your being.
- Maintains virility and fertility.
- Protection – gather on Midsummer Eve and hang over doors and windows. Use a bunch to sprinkle water about the house, doors and windows.
- Reputed to restore lost eyesight.
- Taking fennel as a magical tonic will bring the ability to have a long life filled with the ability to face danger and be strong in the face of adversity.

HAWTHORN

(*Crataegus* spp., *C. monogyna* – Ireland). Irish – Huath, an Sceach Gheal. Perrenial.
Family: Rosacea.
Folknames: Hagthorn, ladies' meat, pixie pears, quickset, maythorn, fairy tree.
Habitat: Native to the Isles and Europe, hawthorn likes to grow near people, along rivers, moist canyons, around edges of meadows, on hilltops and tors in Europe, watching over stone circles.
Parts used: Flowering tops (the end 6 inches of the branches), fruits (picked before the first frost).
Constituents: Flavanoids, saponins, tannins, minerals, ascorbic acid, rutin.
Actions: Astringent, cardiac tonic, relaxes peripheral blood vessels, circulatory tonic, amphoteric, diuretic, hypotensive, digestive tonic.

Hawthorn is completely non-toxic – there are NO side effects or contraindications, and it is complementary with allopathic drugs.

Specific uses

- Improves strength and contraction of heart muscles.
- Opens up arteries, improving blood supply to tissues and organs.
- Balances blood pressure and heartbeat.
- Alleviates congestion and pressure on the heart, lowering chances of heart attack.
- Improves circulation to the brain due to ageing and stress.
- Irregular heartbeat, angina, heart valve disease.
- Diuretic – alleviates fluid retention due to heart/kidney disease.

Applications: Tea: 3 cups a day. Tincture: 3 tsp. a day.

Metaphysical

Plant of Water, the Mother, the Good Folk

The sacred hawthorn can live for 400 years. Protected by her thorns, she provides food and shelter for insects, birds and other wild creatures.

Known as the Fairie Tree, there is a hawthorn growing beside nearly every stone circle in Ireland. The local people, even today, consider it to be extreme ill fortune to cut them down, which would incur the wrath of the Faerie who reside there. Indeed, there are actual recorded incidents of dire consequences falling upon the men who did such a thing in the name of progress! (They died soon after their deed.)

Throughout Celtic Europe, hawthorn has, for thousands of years, been an ally for healing and magic. Blooming in late April/early May, hawthorn is a tree of fertility and is incorporated in Beltain handfasting and wedding rites to symbolise harmony and equality between the masculine and feminine energies. Garlands are woven and worn by the couple and hung over doorways of homes and barns to bring good fortune. The hawthorn trees themselves are decorated at Midsummer with flower garlands and red ribbons, honouring the spirit of the tree and the creatures who dwell there.

Hawthorn strengthens the metaphysical heart and opens the passage-ways to get love flowing. She protects vulnerable emotions and imparts the courage to risk intimacy.

Incorporate hawthorn into your rituals as incense, flower essence, tea and bath herb to heal and strengthen the heart, increase magical vibrations and invoke the blessings of the Good Folk.

HYSSOP

(*Hyssopus off.*).
DO NOT USE IF PREGNANT OR EPILEPTIC!
Family: *Labiatae*. Perrenial.
Habitat: Native of Mediterranean and temperate Asia, naturalised through-out America, Russia and Europe. Dry and sunny. Tolerates most soils.
Constituents: Volatile oil, flavanoids, tannins, bitter.
Actions: Astringent, antiseptic, expectorant, carminative, diuretic, diaphoretic, antispasmodic, anti-viral, febrifuge, reduces phlegm, topical anti-inflammatory, heart and circulatory tonic, nervine, sedative, emmenagogue, vermifuge, vulnerary.

Specific uses

- Colds, flu, bronchitis, sinusitis, respiratory infections.
- *Herpes simplex*.
- Digestive upsets, nervous stomach.
- Burns and bruises, dermatitis, eczema.
- Nervous exhaustion, anxiety, hysteria, melancholy, grief, guilt.
- Rheumatism.
- Regulates blood pressure.

Applications

- Tea – 3 cups a day; or tincture – 3 tsp. a day.
- Incense.
- Aromatherapy – steams, baths and compresses – lightly! High doses of essential oils can cause convulsions!

Metaphysics

Herb of Air.

Hyssop is like a fresh breeze, cleansing the aura and blowing away nega-tivity. Used since ancient times to purify and protect sacred space, hyssop can be hung in bunches around the home to prevent negativity from entering and to raise positive vibrations. Use in the bath or as incense to purify before ritual.

LEMON BALM

(*Melissa off.*). Irish – Lus na Meala.

Family: *Labiatae*.
Parts used: Leaves/flowers.
Habitat: Native of Europe, cultivated in gardens, escaped to disturbed places.
Constituents: essential oil, bitters, flavanoids.
Actions: Calming nervine, anti-microbial, anti-viral, anti-spasmodic, anti-histaminic.

Specific uses

- Insomnia.
- Headaches.
- Depression (especially SAD (seasonal affective disorder) syndrome).
- Digestive disorders.
- Palpitations (nervous).
- Harmonises gall bladder and stomach.
- Relieves flatulence.
- Colds and flus – safe for children and elders.
- Relieves respiratory allergies.

Applications

- 1 Tablespoon fresh herb to 1 cup boiling water infusion – 4 cups day.
- Tincture (fresh) – 20–30 drops 3 times a day.

Add to lotions and creams.

Metaphysical

Herb of Fire, the Sun.

- Attracts what we need to feel nourished.
- An antidote for winter melancholy.
- Increases creative vitality.
- Brings sunlight into the body.
- Aids self-esteem.

MUGWORT

(*Artemesia vulgaris*). Irish – an Mongach Meisce (long-haired intoxication). Perennial.
DO NOT USE DURING PREGNANCY
Folknames: Witch herb, cronewort, Old Man and many others!

Family: Compositae.
Habitat: Native of Europe. Mugwort will grow in most soils, liking full sun and full moonlight. Propagate by cuttings or root division.
Constituents: Volatile oil, flavanoids, bitter principle, coumarins.
Actions: Bitter tonic, nervine tonic, reproductive tonic, emmenagogue, carminative, circulatory stimulant, anti-inflammatory.

Specific uses

- Painful, sluggish menses.
- Nervous tension, hysteria, depression.
- Indigestion, nausea, upset stomach.
- Rheumatism.

Applications

- 1 cup of tea a day or 1 tsp. tincture as a bitter tonic.
- 1–2 cups of tea or 1–2 tsp. of tincture as an emmenagogue.

Metaphysics

Herb of Water, herb of the Triple Goddess, herb of the Moon

Woven into Women's Mystery Rites to represent and invoke the Maiden, Mother and the Crone, mugwort was as sacred to our European foremothers as wild white sage is to indigenous peoples of North America. Mugwort empowers the sacredness of all phases of Womanhood, the Sacred Midwife who aids transformation and rebirth. Watch her in the garden on a windy day. See how gracefully she dances with the breeze, bends with the wind, her long, silver-green leaf hair swirling around her? Go out and sit with her on a Full Moon night. Isn't she gorgeous, as she reflects the Lunar Lady?

In Celtic Midsummer celebrations, girls would wear garlands and girdles of Mugwort for the dance and then throw them into the fire for protection in the coming year.

Mugwort lends her powers to cleanse and empower your divination tools and altar objects. Make a light infusion and apply to increase their magic.

Mugwort can be offered as incense, ritual tea, bath and amulet herb to deepen connection with the Triple Goddess and strengthen Their energies in your Self and your environment.

Add a small amount to dream pillows to stimulate dreaming.

Incorporate mugwort into Rites of Passage rituals for all Women's Blood Mysteries, First Menarch, birth and menopause.

NETTLES

(*Urtica dioica*). Perrenial. Irish – an Neantog.
Folkname: Stinging nettles.
Family: Urticacea.
Habitat: Native to Eurasia and Africa, naturalised elsewhere. Nettles grows by roadsides, edges of woods and waterbanks. There are 500 species.
Parts used: New growth leaves and stems. Collect in the spring. Make fresh tincture in apple cider vinegar or alcohol for asthma. Use dry leaf tea or tincture for nutrient tonic.
Constituents: Chlorophyll, Vitamins A, B complex, C, D, E and K, folic acid, minerals, bioflavanoids, seratonin precursor.
Actions: nutrient, tonic, anti-inflammatory, diuretic, anti-rheumatic, alterative, rubefacient, astringent, haemostatic, circulatory tonic.

Specific uses

Whole body nutrient.

- Reduce fatigue, improve stamina.
- Nourish the kidneys and adrenal glands.
- Nourish the immune system.
- Nourish the digestive system.
- Nourish the endocrine system. Increase metabolism, normalise weight.
- Create strong, flexible bones. Ease/prevent sore joints (rheumatism, arthritis).
- Promote healthy skin/hair.
- Nourish and heal the lower respiratory system.
- Lungs – asthma and allergies (use fresh).

For pregnancy

- Prevents oedema.
- Increases fertility.
- Eases leg cramps and muscle spasms.
- High in calcium – diminishes pain.
- Rich in Vitamin K – increases haemoglobin, prevents haemorrhage after birth.
- Reduces haemorrhoids – tightens/strengthens blood vessels, maintains arterial elasticity, improves resiliency.
- Increases quantity and richness of breast milk.

1 cup three times a day.

Metaphysical

Plant of Earth and Water

Madam Nettle's power is best understood when gathering her fresh leaves and stems. She commands respect. One must approach her with great care and proper etiquette or she will sting! (She also insists that we wear gloves when waiting upon her – she's a bit Victorian that way.) Once we have demonstrated our good manners, she offers us protection, self-respect, resiliency and flexibility. She teaches healthy boundaries while providing deep nourishment.

Use as a meditational tea and bath herb.

PEPPERMINT

(*Mentha piperita*). Irish – Lus an Phiobair.
Folknames: Monk's herb, Our Lady's mint, Sage of Bethlehem, cradle-wort.
Habitat: Cultivated throughout Europe, Asia and North America.
Parts used: Aerial.
Constituents: essential oil (menthol, menthone, menthyl acetate) flavanoids (including rutin), azulene, carotene.
Actions: Carminative, anti-spasmodic, anti-microbial, anti-inflammatory, diaphoretic, anti-emetic, nervine (stimulant), antiseptic, analgesic, brain stimulant, cooling tonic.

Specific uses

- Relaxes muscles of the digestive system, stimulates bile and digestive juices.
- Anaesthetic to the stomach wall.
- Nausea, vomiting, flatulence, colic.
- Fevers, colds, flu.
- Headaches, nervous tension, anxiety.
- Rheumatic pain relief (essential oil).
- Asthma and chronic bronchitis.
- Cuts, bruises, wounds.

Prepared as tea, tincture, oil, glycerite, salve, bath, poultice.
Peppermint is a good synergiser for formulas.

Metaphysics

Herb of Air and Earth

Peppermint helps us to expand and open to cosmic energies.

From the Latin word 'mente' meaning 'thought', peppermint offers purification, protection, prosperity, restoration, renewal and clear thinking.

Anoint green candles with mint oil to draw money – also carry in your wallet. May your prosperity spread as the mint does in the garden!

Peppermint stimulates dreams and visions. Use as a divination tea.

PLANTAIN

(*Plantago lanceolata, P. major*). Irish – Cuach Phádraig (Embrace of Patrick).
Folknames: Waybread (Saxon), Englishman's foot (Native American).
Family: *Plantaginaceae.*
Habitat: temperate regions – Europe, Asia, Africa, everywhere!
Parts used: Leaves, seeds.
Constituents: Leaves: mucilage, glycosides, tannins, silicic acid, minerals. Seeds, leaves: mucilage, oils, protein, starch.
Actions: Anti-inflammatory, demulcent, astringent, diuretic, relaxing expectorant, anti-spasmodic.
Seeds: Demulcent, laxative.

Specific uses

- Cystitis – soothes urinary tract infections.
- Inflammation of upper respiratory passages, reduces phlegm.
- Bronchitis.
- Digestive disorders, intestinal worms.
- Haemorrhoids, diarrhoea.
- Slow healing wounds.
- Bites, bruises, swelling.
- Cysts.

Specific uses – fresh or dry.

- 1 tsp. to 1 cup water infusion.
- Tincture – 20 drops 3 times a day.
- External wash or poultice.

Metaphysical

Plant of Fire, plant of the Warrior.

Plantain is written of in the ancient Saxon 'Nine Herbs Charm':

And you, waybread,
  mother of herbs,
Open from eastward,
  Mighty within
Over you carts creaked,
  Over you queens rode,
Over you brides travelled,
  Over you, bulls breathed,
All you withstood, and stopped, astonished,
As you withstand venom and flying ills
And loathsome ones that fare through the land.

Plantain offers protection when we are moving through challenge and helps us reach the goal, empowering us to withstand negativity and remain constant upon the path.

Carry in a charm bag to aid healing of grief and sorrow.

Meditate with plantain to receive visions of the future.

RED CLOVER

(*Trifolium pratense*). Irish – na seamra rua. Annual.
Folknames: Three-leaved grass, meadow trefoil.
Family: *Leguminosae*.
Habitat: Native of Europe. Likes moist, grassy places, cultivated land. Red clover makes a great cover crop to prevent soil erosion and provide nutrients.
Parts used: Flowers – May to September.
Constituents: (Phenolic and cyanogenic) glycosides, flavanoids, salicylates, coumarins, vitamins and minerals.
Actions: Alterative, antispasmodic, diuretic, anti-inflammatory, anti-coagulant, anti-tumour, possible oestrogenic, nutrient.

Specific uses

- Cleansing for skin complaints – eczema and psoriasis.
- Stubborn, dry coughs.
- Arthritis and gout.
- Jaundice, hepatitis, mononucleosis.
- Ulcers and burns – salve and/or poultice.
- Mastitis – inflammation.
- Cancerous growths: throat – gargle w/tea 4–5 times a day. Stomach – 4 cups of tea a day on an empty stomach.

- Ovarian/uterine cysts.

Do not use long term without breaks – 3 weeks on, 1week off.
   Do not use with prescription drugs. It thins the blood.

In the garden

Red clover is an excellent cover and forage crop, fixing nitrogen in the soil. It provides green manure – sow seeds in the autumn to provide winter cover. Then in the spring, simply turn it into the soil for lots of lovely nutrients. Bees love this plant!

Metaphysics

Herb of Earth, herb of Air, herb of Contemplation

Plant of prosperity. Dispels melancholy.
   3 leaf = The Trinity – Maiden, Mother Crone; Earth, Sky and Sea, etc.
   4 leaf = Love, fame, health and wealth – the four elements.
   Add to the bath for success in and being granted any monetary favour.
   As a flower essence, it brings calm in the midst of group panic.

ROSE

(*Rosa* spp., wild rose – *Rosa canina*). Perennial. Irish – an Ros. Wild rose (an Fheirdhris)
Family: Rosacea.
Habitat: All temperate regions of the world, probably first cultivated in Persia, Greece, Italy.
Parts used: Flowers, leaves, fruit (rosehips), essential oil.
Constituents: volatile oils, tannins, Vitamins C, B, E, K, flavanoids, mucilage, saponins, bitters.
Actions: antidepressant, antispasmodic, aphrodisiac, astringent, sedative, digestive stimulant, bile stimulant, expectorant, anti-microbial, anti-viral, antiseptic, kidney tonic, blood tonic, menstrual regulator, anti-inflammatory, nervine tonic.

Specific uses:

- Strengthens the heart – counters tremblings, swooning, fainting.
- Emollient for skin.
- Gargle for mouth sores, throat.

- Inflammation of eyes, ears, throat and gums.
- Insomnia, depression, irritability.
- Restorative to nervous system.
- Strengthens capillaries and connective tissue.
- Menstrual regulator.
- Digestive balancer.

Applications

- Leaf and flower tea – 1 cup 3 times a day
- Use rosewater in lotions, creams and baths to heal and beautify the skin.

Rosehips (*Fructus cynodhati*) – from *Rosa canina* (wild rose).
Habitat: Temperate regions of Europe, Asia, Africa. Harvest after first frost.
Constituents: tannins, sugars, organic acids, vitamins A, B1, B2, C (3 hips=1 orange), E, K, carotenoids, calcium, iron, silica.
Actions: Diuretic, tonic, mild laxative, regenerating, anti-bacterial.

Specific uses

- Prevention of flu and diseases associated with chilling – coughs and colds.
- Convalescent recovery.
- Anaemia – stimulates production of red blood cells.
- Cramps and uterine difficulties.
- Colic and chronic diarrhoea.
- Urinary tract infections.
- One of the best sources of vitamin C.
- Tonic for general debility and exhaustion.
- Nutritive to nervous and immune systems.
- Heart and circulatory tonic.

Applications

- Decoction of 1 tsp. crushed fruit to 1 cup water 4–6 times a day.
- 1 tsp. of tincture 4–6 times a day.

Rosewater

On a warm sunny morning, gather enough rose petals to fill a sterilised quart jar. Cover with pure spring water and leave in a warm place for 3 days. Strain and refrigerate until needed. You can also buy distilled rose-water.

Rosehip syrup

Make a decoction of rosehips. Strain and add an equal amount of honey. Take 3 times a day for a full quotient of Vitamin C. Great for children and they love it!

Metaphysical

Plant of Water. Love! Heart!

Madam Rose aids heart healing due to loss and rejection, increases compassion and unconditional love and helps to soften and open a 'bitter' heart.

Rose promotes self-love and sacred sensuality, increasing enjoyment of Earthly life.

Truly a queen, she is a powerful archetype for women as she allows her beauty to fully bloom while her thorns command healthy boundaries of respect. No wonder she is associated with all the Goddesses of love and beauty!

SAGE

(*Salvia off.*). Irish – an saiste.
Family: Labiatae.
Habitat: Native of the Mediterranean, widely cultivated in gardens everywhere. Sage needs full sun and likes a bit of sand in the soil.
Parts used: Leaves and flowers.
Constituents: Flavanoids, phytosterols, calcium, magnesium, potassium, zinc, thiamine, saponins, essential fatty acids, essential oils, carotenes, tannins, antioxidants, bitter, resin.
Actions: Antiseptic, anti-microbial, nutritive tonic, anti-inflammatory, astringent (very!), carminative, anti-spasmodic.

Grandmother Sage has bestowed her healing properties on humanity, especially Elders, throughout history. Definitely a potent effector herb, sage should be used in small amounts, for short periods of time. Her power goes a long way.

- Reduces hot flushes and night sweats.
- Oestrogenic balancer.
- Anti-depressant – due to rich minerals.
- Relieves dizziness, trembling, emotional swings – again, due to depleted minerals.

- Relieves headaches and aching joints.
- Liver and digestive tonic.
- Carminative – relieves gas and nausea.
- Relieves menstrual cramps and flooding.
- Urinary disinfectant for bladder infections.
- Improves circulation.
- Tonic for Elders.

Application: 1 tsp. dried leaf infusion with honey, 1 cup a day; or 20 drops fresh leaf tincture 3 times a week. Do not use if experiencing dry mouth or vagina.

Metaphysics

Herb of Earth, herb of the Crone.

The Romans bestowed the name 'salvia', meaning 'I save'.

'Sage' is the title we give to a wise person.

Sage is like the wise Grandmother who offers her grounding experience and unconditional love, while she dries our tears and mops up all kinds of wet conditions. She is able to nourish and heal with her micro-nutrients and essential oils.

Sage will purify the environment and ground erratic energies, within us and around us.

She helps us to connect with our ancestors and avail of their wisdom.

The Chinese people so revered the healing properties of European sage that they traded 3 boxes of their tea for 1 box of sage!

Weave sage into your life as incense, ritual tea, bath and amulet herb. Hang bunches around the house for the Crone's blessings.

THYME

(*Thymus vulgaris*). Irish – an Tim. Perennial. Thymus = the courage to be.
Family: Labiatae.
Habitat: cultivated in gardens. Native to the Mediterranean and southern Europe.
Parts used: Leaves/flowers.
Constituents: essential oil (+3%), thymol, carvaerol, cineol, tannins, saponins, bitters, glycosides, flavanoids.
Actions: the strongest anti-microbial, anti-bacterial, anti-fungal, antiseptic, antispasmodic, expectorant, astringent, digestive stimulant, anti-tussive, diuretic, rubefacient.

Specific uses

- Upper respiratory diseases, dissolves mucus, relieves bronchial spasms, antiseptic, expectorant, antispasmodic (essential oil excretes through the lungs, alleviates symptoms of emphysema and asthma).
- Digestive disorders and flatulence, anorexia/bulimia, antiseptic and antispasmodic to the intestinal walls, stimulates appetite.
- Dermatological agent – stubborn rashes, scabies, athlete's foot, ringworm.
- Relieves tired muscles and exhaustion and melancholy.
- Incredible infection fighter – immune strengthener, stimulates the thymus gland.
- Arthritis.

Applications: 1 tsp. herb to 1 cup boiling water 3 times a day. Tincture: 1 tsp. in 1 cup water 3 times a day. Chest rub: 5 drops in 1 oz. carrier oil, also apply to insect bites and wounds. Mouthwash and gargle: use strong tea. Thyme in cooking protects from *E. coli*, *salmonella*, etc. Use 10 drops thyme essential oil and 10 drops lemon essential oil in a 12 oz. spray bottle of water as a powerful disinfectant in the kitchen and bathroom.

Metaphysical

A plant of Air

One of the fairies' favourites. Used in magical recipes, it gives us the vision to see them. Planted in the garden, it invites them to dwell with us.

- Carry to ensure your actions are praised and your style admired.
- Bestows graceful elegance.
- Use to increase or shorten 'time' in your life – be specific.
- Bestows courage – knights wore sprigs of it into battle in the Middle Ages.
- Romans burned it to repel scorpions.
- Use to improve and facilitate communication.
- Bee plant.

Druid incense – combine with Juniper for vision.

Fairy incense:

- Thyme.
- Elder flowers.
- Calendula flowers.

- Foxglove flowers.

Add to cleansing baths – very antiseptic. Use sparingly! Very potent!

VERVAIN

(*Verbena off.*). Irish: an Bheirbheine. Fer faen (to drive away/stone).
Perennial.
Folk names: Enchanters herb, holy herb, van van. Sacred to the Druids,
wizard's plant. The Romans called it 'hiera botane' (sacred plant).
Family: *Verbenaceae*.
Parts used: Aerial parts.
Habitat: Full sun. Native of Europe.
Constituents: Bitter glycosides: verbenalin (mild purgative) and verbenin,
essential oil, mucilage, tannins.
Actions: Nervine, relaxant tonic, galactagogue, diaphoretic, sedative, anti-
spasmodic, liver restorative, digestive laxative, uterine stimulant and
cleanser, bile stimulant, febrifuge, vulnerary, anti-depressant, anti-inflammatory, digestive, nervous system and blood tonic.

Applications

- Insomnia, nervous tension.
- Encourage sweating.
- Poor appetite and digestive function.
- Encourages contractions during labour.
- Nervous exhaustion and depression.
- Toxic conditions, e.g. jaundice.
- External – bites, sprains, bruises, eczema, wounds, open sores, neur-
algia.
- Mouth ulcers, spongy gums, tonsillitis.
- Liver and gallbladder disease.
- Migraine and nervous headaches.
- Tests have shown possible heart-strengthening and anti-tumour
activity.

Application: One cup a day, sipped throughout the day, for an adult.
Avoid in pregnancy, except during labour. Emetic in high doses.

Metaphysical

When burned, vervain wards off psychic attack, purifies, attracts love and
wealth, friendship, joy and good luck.

One of the three most sacred herbs to the Celts and their Druids, who included their revered ally in all their seasonal, divination and healing rituals, as incense and lustral water to prepare the altar and to invoke the Divine. It was ceremonially gathered with the left hand, when neither the Sun or Moon were in the sky, leaving a libation of honey in thanks to the spirit of the plant. The tea was partaken of before ritual to heighten consciousness and intensify clairvoyant powers, and the bardic poet singers drank it to receive inspiration. The Celts held vervain with the same reverence as the indigenous peoples of the American continent hold wild white sage. Vervain forms the core of most of my sacred recipes. I use it in my home daily for all its blessings.

Bards were initiated with the brew from Cerridwen's Cauldron, bestowing eloquence, inspiration, prophecy and song. It contained:

- Rowan berries.
- Sea water (also used in the ritual drink of 'The mysteries of Ceres').
- Lesser celandine (Taliesin's cresses – ficaria).
- Flixweed (*Descurainia sophia* – Gwion's Silver).
- Vervain.

The Romans considered it sacred to Venus.

The Greeks perceived it as sacred to Aphrodite.

The Pawnee used it to enhance dreams.

Christian tradition told that it grew on Mount Calvary and was used to staunch Christ's wounds.

The Persians held bunches of vervain while facing the Sun to greet the new day.

The Egyptians said that it formed from the Tears of Isis.

Mothers gave vervain in amulet form to their children to make them quick learners, and hung it over their beds for protection and to prevent nightmares. Warriors carried vervain to help them escape their enemies, farmers buried it in their fields to ensure bountiful harvests, and lovers used it to bring about union with the beloved.

The healers of the Celts honoured and worked with Vervain to bring about the healing of the physical body. They understood vervain's actions as a relaxing nervine, a digestive tonic, an antidepressant and wound healer. It was an ally during times of fever, due to its diaphoretic, febrifuge and alterative gifts.

Thought to be so kindly disposed toward human beings, it would only grow within a mile of human habitation. Vervain is very easy to grow in your gardens. She likes full Sun and moderate watering. At twilight (when neither the Sun nor Moon are in the sky), gather the top 8 inches

212

when they come into flower. Leave a gift and hang bundles of the plant upside down in a warm, dark place to dry. For incense and other magical recipes, I use flower, leaf and stem; for medicine, I use the flower and leaf.

- Hang bunches in the home or burn as incense to protect against negativity, lightning, storms. Also sprinkled around the house.
- Use in the ritual bath to detoxify and cleanse the aura.

It is said that vervain will bring magical powers and immortality to its possessor!

- Totem animal – the hawk.

Journey on her wings and receive the messages and omens only her clear eyes can detect. If you need to examine your life from a greater perspective, use vervain as your ally.

Use vervain infused oil to consecrate the third eye and tools for divination.

VITEX

(*Vitex agnus-castus*).
DO NOT USE DURING PREGNANCY OR BREASTFEEDING
Folknames: Chasteberry, Monk's Pepper.
Family: Verbenaceae.
Habitat: Native of the Mediterranean and North Africa. Vitex needs full sun, sandy soil and lots of water. She doesn't do well in Northern climates, unless you keep her indoors.
Parts used: Berries.
Constituents: Flavanoids, glycosides, volatile oils, bitter principle.

Actions

- Female reproductive tonic and hormonal balancer, anti-microbial, anti-inflammatory, astringent, bitter tonic and digestive stimulant, anti-fibroid.
- Affects the pituitary gland to restore oestrogen and progesterone balance.
- Eases pre-menstrual tension. (However, there's nothing vitex can do about societal attitudes or stresses, which are the main cause and what need to be worked on and changed.)
- Regulates menstruation, alleviates endometriosis and other issues of infertility.
- Reduces and eliminates fibroid cysts.

- Relieves chronic menstrual cramps (combined with not wearing tampons).
- Reduces and eliminates menopausal imbalances, including severe hot flushes, lowered libido, spotting, flooding, sleep disturbances. Again, societal attitudes apply.
- Clears skin problems that are due to hormonal imbalance.
- Relieves hormone-related constipation and digestive sluggishness.
- Provides slow, steady grounding and stamina (consistent, elegant energy).
- Protects against osteoporosis.
- Reverses dry vaginal tissue.
- Reduces/eliminates hormone-related migraines.

Applications
- 20 drops of tincture, 1–2 times a day.
- 3 capsules of ground berries daily.
- 1 tsp. of ground berries, used as 'pepper' daily.

Metaphysics

Herb of Venus, herb of Fire

Vitex provides energy, rejuvenation and renewed vitality. She blesses us with new passion and inspiration. She offers her fire when we have been 'burnt out'.

Vitex is the herb that the Great Goddess Hera herself took to prepare for her three-hundred year-long honeymoon with Zeus! Talk about providing sexual stamina!

She helps all women to find their sassy, spunky, peppery, spicy side!

Use as incense, amulet ingredient and Fire offering.

YARROW

(*Achillea millefolium*). Irish – an Athair Thalun. Perennial.
AVOID IN PREGNANCY
Family: Compositae.
Parts used: Leaf and flower.
Habitat: Native in Europe and Asia; introduced in North America, Australia, New Zealand; high mountains with pines, river valleys.
Constituents: Volatile oil, bitter, tannins, coumarins, amino acids, flavanoids.

Actions: Tonic, alterative, diaphoretic, diuretic, astringent, antiseptic, vulnerary, styptic, bitter, anti-inflammatory, febrifuge, anti-allergenic, anti-spasmodic, uterine stimulant.

Systems affected: Cardiovascular, circulatory, digestive, genito-urinary, skin.

- Lowers vasodilator blood pressure and tones blood vessels.
- Raises, moderates body heat, equalises circulation, produces perspiration.
- Urinary infections.
- Colds, flus, fevers – child safe.
- Stimulates appetite.
- Yeast infections – candida.

Dosage

- Cold infusion – for incontinence.
- Warm infusion – for cramping, infections, etc.
- Tonic – 1 cup tea per day.
- 1 dropper tincture 3 times a day.
- Infections – 1 cup tea or 1 tsp. tincture 4–6 times a day.

Can cause faintness, skin irritation.

Metaphysical

Plant of Fire

Yarrow invokes the God and the Warrior and empowers the masculine. In an amulet, it bestows confidence, determination and faith in one's own healing abilities.

It is added to dream potions to meet one's lover on the ethereal plane.

Gods, Demons and Symbols of Ancient Mesopotamia
Jeremy Black & Anthony Green
British Museum Press, 1992

Beaunacht Bhride leat!

DARK MOON DESIGNS

Dark Moon Designs are taken from the original paintings of Jane Brideson and inspired by the cycle of the seasons, the moon and our sacred earth.

Our range of full colour cards and prints includes the eight festivals of the Wheel of the Year, Celtic Goddesses and Gods, Green Men, Lunar Cycle and many more.

For a full colour catalogue please send a cheque/postal order for £4.00 or $6.00 made payable to DARK MOON DESIGNS to the address below. Alternatively you can visit our website at: www.darkmoondesigns.net

Dark Moon Designs,
Rainbow Cottage,
Clonduff,
Rosenallis,
Co. Laois
Republic of Ireland
Email: morrigan@mac.com